STATISTICAL ACCOUNT OF JUNAGADH

STATISTICAL ACCOUNT OF JUNAGADH

BEING THE JUNAGHADH CONTRIBUTION TO THE KATHIAWAR PORTION OF THE BOMBAY GAZETTEER

WATSON, J. W.

GYAN

Published by

GYAN

Gyan Publishing House
5, Ansari Road
Daryaganj, New Delhi-110002
Phone: 011-47034999, 9811692060
E-mail: books@gyanbooks.com

Distribution Network
gyanbooks.com
India, USA, Canada, UK, Australia

ISBN: 978-93-7169-247-2 (HB)

First Published, 1884

2nd Impression 2026

Printed at: Gyan Press, Delhi.

STATISTICAL ACCOUNT OF JUNAGADH

Author: WATSON, J. W.

STATISTICAL ACCOUNT

OF

JÚNÁGADH;

BEING

THE JÚNÁGADH CONTRIBUTION

TO THE

KATHIAWAR PORTION OF THE BOMBAY GAZETTEER.

BY

COLONEL J. W. WATSON,

PRESIDENT, RÁJASTHÁNIK COURT, KÁTHIÁWÁR.

BOMBAY:

PRINTED AT THE BOMBAY GAZETTE STEAM PRESS, RAMPART ROW.

1884.

CONTENTS.

CHAPTER I.—*Description, Products, and Population.* PAGE

(1) Description :—

Position and Area; Boundaries; Aspect; Hills; Geological Formations; Rivers; Lakes and Reservoirs; Wells and Water Supply; Soil; Climate 1

(2) Products :—

Forests and Trees; Plantations; Crops; Mode of Cultivation; Domestic Animals; Wild Animals; Sea Produce—Pearls, Coral 4

(3) Population :—

Census Details; Aboriginal and other Tribes; Religion; Occupation; Mode of Living; Language; Houses; Number of Villages 7

CHAPTER II.—*Trade.*

(1) Trade :—

Principal Ports; Description; Shipping; Course of Trade 11

(2) Salt Manufacture :—

Salt and Salt Works; Amount Annually produced; Share of Revenue accruing to Durbar... 16

(3) Money Lending :—

Banking; Kori Coinage; Gold Coins; Prices; Table of Wages; Weights and Measures 16

CHAPTER III.—*History* 21

PAGE

CHAPTER IV.—*Details of Administration.*

(1) Land :—

Land Tenure—Khálsáh and Bárkháli Lands; Pasáitá, Dharmádá, Jivái, Inámi, Patel Palat, and Service Tenures; Kapál Grás, Múlgrás; Tenant Proprietors under the State; Tenant Proprietors under the Vassals; Land whether or not liable to Debt; Land Revenue how collected; Collection of Arrears how enforced...... 62

(2) Justice :—

Criminal Courts; Civil Courts; Appellate Courts; Working of the Courts; Miscellaneous Departments; Internal Management of Vassal Villages; Incidence of the Land Tax; State Demand how levied....... 64

(3) Police and Military 67

(4) Revenue and Finance 68

(5) Customs and Transit Dues........................ 69

(6) Miscellaneous Cesses 70

(7) Education 71

(8) Sanitary 72

(9) Public Works 72

CHAPTER V.—*Towns and Places of Interest* (containing a detailed account of the History of the Chudásamás) 74

General Statement showing the Import and Export of Goods in the Samwat Years 1906, 1926, and 1933 (1849-50, 1869-70, and 1876-77 A.D.) 161

Banner,

PRESENTED TO

H. H. SIR MAHABAT KHANJI, K.C.S.I.,

NAWAB OF JUNAGADH,

On 1st January 1877,

BY HIS EXCELLENCY

LORD LYTTON, G.M.S.I. &C. &C.

VICEROY AND GOVERNOR GENERAL OF INDIA.

On the occasion of the Imperial Assemblage at Delhi to celebrate the assumption of the Title of "KAISAR-I-HIND" (EMPRESS OF INDIA) by Her most Gracious Majesty Queen Victoria.

ARMORIAL BEARINGS OF H. H. THE NAWAB OF JUNAGADH.

Arms.—On a field vert three bezants between three rocks proper.

Crest.—A lion's face, affronté, proper, langue gules.

Supporters.—Two lions, argent rampant.

Motto.—[illegible]: or, on a scroll, azure, from which is suspended the Most Exalted Order of the Star of India.

HIS HIGHNESS
MAHABAT KHAN, K.C.S.I.
NAWAB OF JUNAGADH

JÚNÁGADH.

CHAPTER I.

DESCRIPTION, PRODUCTS, AND POPULATION.

Position and area.

The State of Júnágadh lies to the south-west of the peninsula of Káthiáwár. It lies between 24° 44′ and 21° 53′ north latitude, and 70° and 72° east longitude. Its area is about 3,283 square miles, with a population, according to the census of 1881, of 387,409 souls. A map is attached.

Boundaries.

The State is bounded on the north by the Bardá, Hálár, and Káthiáwár proper sub-divisions of the province, on the east by Gohelwár and Káthiáwár, and on the west and south by the Arabian Sea. The Júnágadh State is divided into twenty maháls, viz., those of (1) Uná, (2) Sútrápádá, (3) Pátan, (4) Veráwal, (5) Chorwár, (6) Máliá, (7) Kesoj, (8) Wanthali, (9) Bálágám, (10) Sil, (11) Maḥiári, (12) Kútiáná, (13) Wadál, (14) Nawágadh-Jetpúr, (15) Bhensán, (16) Visáwadar, (17) Bagḍú, (18) Mángrol, (19) Ránpúr, and (20) Khaḍia. Júnágadh itself is included in no mahál but is a separate charge.

Aspect.

The aspect of the country is, as a rule, hilly, although there are extensive plains of exceedingly rich soil. The highest range of hills is that of Mount Girnár, while the largest and most widely extended range is that in the Gir District. The highest peak of the Girnár itself is that of Gorak-náth, 3,666 feet. The Dátár mountain in the same group is 2,779, while the hills of Láso-Páwaḍi and Bhenslá of the same cluster

Hills.

are 2,527 and 2,290 feet respectively. The principal peaks in the Júnágadh portion of the Gir are as follows :—

Karakio,	1,946	feet,	in the vicinity of Visáwadar.
Dúndi,	1,584	„	in the Cheluá limits.
Lápála,	1,547	„	in the Visáwadar limits.
Rozmál,	1,525	„	in the neighbourhood of Máliá.
Hadálidhár,	1,552	„	in the Uná Parganah.
Sáyo,	1,574	„	in the Pátan Gir.
Ratno,	1,623	„	in the limits of Chelná.

Geological formations.

All the hills are volcanic and consist of trap and basalt piercing through and elevating limestone. But the summit of the Girnár is composed of syenite, which is to be found in the Girnár clump and elsewhere ; and in the small isolated hill of Dátráná, stone of excellent quality is obtainable. The Gírnár clump are as a rule thickly wooded, and there are miles of excellent forest in the Gir district, though from want of proper supervision but little revenue is realized from them.

Rivers.

The principal rivers are the Bhádar, Uben, Ojat, Hiran, Sarasvati, Machûndri, Singávaḍá, Megal, Vrajni, and Ráwal. Of these the Uben and Ojat fall into the Bhádar which is the largest river in the province, and much irrigation is carried on along its banks, and the banks of its tributaries. The Hiran, Ráwal, Singávaḍá, Megal, Vrajni, and Machûndri flow for the greater part of their course through the Gir district, and the Sarasvati or sacred river of Prabhás Pátan is famous in the sacred annals of the Hindus.

Lakes and Reservoirs.

There are numerous tanks and reservoirs of water, the largest of which is the Mohotá Taláv, built by Sardárkhán at the capital. There is another of the same name in Pátan Somnáth, and one of the name of Chitrásar in the Uná parganah. The lake called Sarowardú, situated near the village of the same name in Bábriáwár. The Lánch tank near Dhámlej in Nágher. The Bhúwaḍ tank near Bhúwá Timbá in Bábriáwár. The Dhandúsar tank near the village of the same name north-west of Júnágadh. The Bhálká Taláv between Veráwal and Pátan. The Bháthrot tank near Sil famous for its red and white lotuses, and the Mitiálá tank also near this town.

Wells and water supply.

There are in all in the Júnágadh State 10,158 wells used for purposes of irrigation, out of these 5,058 are built of masonry, the rest are only temporary. Water is found universally near the surface, the deepest well in the State nowhere exceeding 50 feet except in the city of Júnágadh itself. Water is found at a depth of from 6 to 10 feet in Bábriáwár and Uná and elsewhere.

Soil.

The soil is divided into numerous classes, but for practical purpose there are but three kinds, viz., garden and dry crop land and rice land. There is a fourth kind of land called gher or low-lying land extending to 8 or 10 miles from the seashore. This is liable to be inundated during the rainy season and assumes the appearance of a vast swamp. Certain portions of the gher are covered with water till the end of March or April, this land is called Rel; other portions are only covered during the flood time and speedily dry, this land is called Chel. The gher land is twice as productive as ordinary land. Mag, arad, wheat, gram, jowar, coriander seed, castor oil, and cotton are sown in Chel land; and in Rel land mag, arad, and jowár after the water dries up. As a rule the gher is more productive during scanty rains provided at least one flood may have inundated the land. Theg (*cyperus jemenicus*) and Kásiá are produced here spontaneously and eaten by the poorer classes. The principal gher land in Júnágadh territory is that of Bálágám, Bagasrá, Sil, Mahiári, and Kútiáná.

The most fertile portion of the Júnágadh territory is a long strip of land along the coast extending from Mádhavpúr to Uná called Nágher. In this three crops are realized annually, and 300 maunds of gúr are obtainable per acre of sugar-cane.

The climate of the Júnágadh districts is most various, and it possesses on the one hand the salubrious climate of the sea coast and the summit of the lofty hills of Girnár and Dátár, and on the other the hot climate of the plains and the unhealthy climate of the Gir forest. The thermometric readings at Júnágadh show a mean minimum of 58° in the month of January and a mean maximum of 105° in the month of May. But Júnágadh itself is always hot, and on the whole the climate of the town is unhealthy. The average rainfall of Júnágadh from recorded observations for the last four years is 34 inches, but in 1878 there was an exceptional fall of 104·42 inches.

Climate.

The forests of Gir and Girnár are both extensive and valuable. The Gir forest is about 60 miles long by 20 miles in extreme breadth and consists of about 1,000 square miles, of which 800 are in Júnágadh territory. The forest contains numerous hamlets and villages and supports great numbers of cattle which are annually sent hither in the rainy season returning to their homes in about the month of October or November. Large numbers of cattle, however, permanently reside in this forest, which is one of the few remaining haunts of the lion in India; panther, sámbar, chital, and ravine deer are also found here, but neither the bear, bison, nor tiger have ever been known to exist herein. The following are the principal trees :—

Forests and Trees.

1. Ság .... Teak .... *Tectona Grandis.*
2. Sisam .... Blackwood .... *Dalbergia Sissoo.*
3. Timbarwo ... Timru .... *Diospyros Montana.*
4. Kher .... *Acacia Catechu.*
5. Sájar .... *Terminalia glabra.*
6. Bedá .... *Terminalia bellerica.*
7. Ráyan .... *Mimusops hexandrus.*
8. Jámbúdo ...... Jámbu .... *Eugenia Jambolana.*
9. Báwal .... Bábul .... *Acacia Arabica.*
10. Limbdo ...... Nimb .... *Azadirachta Indica.*
11. Bordi .... Ber .... *Zizyphus Jujuba.*

12. Sálera .... *Boswellia thurifera.*
13. Kadáya .... *Sterculia Urens.*
14. Gaṛmálá .... *Cassia Fistula.*
15. Pípal .... Peepul .... *Ficus religiosa.*
16. Waḍ .... Banyan .... *Ficus Indica.*
17. Umro .... Wild Fig Tree ... *Ficus Glomerátá.*
18. Kalam .... *Nauclea parvifolia.*
19. Kadam .... *Nauclea cadamba.*
20. Khijdo .... *Acacia leucophlœa.*
21. Pipar .... *Ficus virens.*
22. Ekal Kántá .... *Alangium Lamarckii.*
23. Semlo .... *Bombax Malabaricum.*
24. Karanj .... *Pongamia glabra.*
25. Ál .... *Morinda citrifolia.*
26. Aritá .... *Sapindus Emarginatus.*
27. Bili .... *Ægle Marmelos.*
28. Kot .... *Feronia Elephantum.*
29. Haldarwo .... *Nauclea Cordifolia.*
30. Saragwo .... *Moringa pterygo sperma.*
31. Ratánjali...... Red Sandal Tree... *Ptero carpus santalinus.*
32. Gúgal .... East Indian Myrrh. *Commiphora Madagascareusis.*
33. Pangárá .... *Erythrina Indica.*
34. Khákhro .... *Butea frondosa.*
35. Jhinjhriá Khákhro .... *Erythrina suberosa.*
36. Rúkhḍo .... *Adansonia digitata.*
37. Sisoti ....
38. Ámli .... Tamarind .... *Tamarindus Indica.*
39. Bolsari .... *Mimusops Elengi.*
40. Babakheri .... *Acacia Farnesiana.*

Plantations. There are large groves of mango trees both in the city of Júnágadh and at Máliá and other places, amd numerous foreign fruits are being grown in the Shakar Bágh at the capital. Amongst these are the lichi, quince, apple, and various kinds of Bombay mangoes. The betel grown at Chorwád in Júnágadh territory is famous not only in the peninsula but also in Gújarát whither it is largely imported.

Crops.

The principal crops of the Júnágadh districts are jowár, bájro, wheat, arad, mag, gram, oil-seed, banti, chino, Indian-corn, cotton, methi, oliá, sugarcane, tobacco, and rice. Verâwal is famous for a large species of onion somewhat resembling the Spanish onion.

Mode of cultivation.

The mode of cultivation in the Júnágadh districts differs in no way from that obtaining elsewhere in the peninsula. Cotton is not, however, raised by irrigation as is customary in Gohelwár and Jháláwár.

Domestic animals.

The domestic animals of the Júnágadh districts are the elephant, the cow, the buffalo, the horse, the ass, the camel, the goat, the sheep, the dog, and the cat. The cows of the Júnágadh districts are famous milkers and the buffaloes are also good. The horses, too, of these parts are good, though inferior to Káthiáwár proper. Bullocks are used of the country breeds, but are also imported from Wadhiár, Sindh, and Wágaḍh. Elephants are only used in State processions.

Wild animals.

The most famous of the wild animals is the lion, who is known by the local name of Sáwaj, the lioness being called Sinhau, the Sanskrit name for lioness. Sáwaj is probably a word of Arabic derivation, meaning he who causes the flocks to bleat. The lion is in no way inferior either in size or courage to the African species, and although the mane is not so large as that of the African lion, is frequently of fair size, and black, tawny, or yellow according to age. The lion is not commonly addicted to man-eating, but I have heard of one or two well authenticated instances, and Captain Jackson and I saw an unfortunate Wághri who had been seized when lying on his bed in a village in the Gir; he was rescued, but died subsequently of his wounds. Two lions frequently hunt together, and a pair so hunting are called a Belár. Even three or more hunt together sometimes. The panther, pig, wolf, hyæna, jackal, and fox abound, as do the nylghau, antelope, and gazelle, though not in such large numbers as formerly. The wild monkey (*Presbytis Entellus*) is fairly frequent in the Gir and Girnár, but in much smaller numbers than in Gújarát. The lynx, manis, and chitáh are occasionally found, and sámbar, chital, and ravine deer reside in the Gir. Sámbar and revine deer also inhabit the Girnár. Porcupines and badgers are also plentiful, though the latter from its nocturnal habits is rarely seen. In the cold weather flocks of "cullum" (*kulang*) of two kinds, viz. (1) *Grus cinerea* and (2) *Authropoides virgo* visit these districts, while the Ghed land swarms with wild duck and teal of various kinds.

Sea Produce.
Pearls.
Coral.

Pearls are occasionally found in the oysters of the Bherái creek, but not in sufficient numbers to render a pearl fishery remunerative. Coral is also found in small quantities at Sil. Mangrove grows at Bherái, but in inconsiderable quantities. Shells of ordinary kinds are found at Sil. Fish and large turtle abound on the coast, and are sometimes, though rarely, caught, but this branch of industry is much neglected, and a large income thereby lost to the State.

Census details.

Of the total population of 387,499, 79 per cent. were Hindús, 19·7 per cent. Músalmáns, and 1·2 were Jains. The number of males was 202,204 or 52·181 per cent. of the whole population, and that of females 185,295 or 47·8 per cent. The average proportion of males to females was 1 to ·916. The number of insane and idiots was 83 or ·0214 per cent., and of lepers was 109 or ·028 per cent. of the whole population.

Aboriginal and other tribes.

The aboriginal tribes consist of Áhirs, Khánts, Kolis, and Káthis of the Wálá and Khúmán tribes. There are also Mers, Mahiás, Hátis; and Rájputs of the Chúḍásamá, Wájá, and other tribes. There are a few Gándharvas who formerly were very numerous, and there are Girnára, Sompará, Patiálá, Gadhiá, and Únewál Bráhmans; also Sorathiá Wániás, and Lohánás, which last are said to have come from Sindh with Rá Noghan on the occasion of his invasion of that country.

Religion.

The Hindú population belong to the following sects :—

Hindú Religious Divisions.

Vaishnavas.					Shaivas.		Mixed.			
Rámánújas.	Valabháchárya.	Kabir Panthis.	Mádhavácháryas.	Swámi Náráyans.	Shankar Smártas.	Lingáyats.	Ascetics or Religious Mendicants.	All who worship simply some god or goddess, &c. &c.	Jains or Shráwaks.	Total.
1	2	3	4	5	6	7	8	9	10	11
4,907	128,124	4,247	21	88,723	6,285	67	2,527	71,394	4,750	311,045

Of the 96,401 Músalmáns, 68,993 are Súnis and 7,408 Shiás. The Pársis and Christians are 30 and 23 respectively.

Occupation.

The census returns for 1881 divided the population into seven classes—(1) persons in State employ or under other local authorities, 8,549 souls, or 2·206 per cent.; (2) domestic servants—6,568 or 1·694 per cent.; (3) mercantile professions 7,738 souls or 1·996 per cent.; (4) persons engaged with agriculture, pasture, or with animals, 131,365 or 33·90 per cent.; (5) persons engaged in industrial pursuits 37,488 or 9·674 per cent.; (6) persons dealing in petty trades, &c., 44,053 or 11·369 per cent.; (7) miscellaneous persons not classed otherwise—(*a*) males 52,685 or 13·593 per cent., and (*b*) females 99,053 or 25·562 per cent. Kumbhárs, Bhois, Báwás, and Mehmans here follow sometimes the occupation of masons and quarry men. Weavers (wankars) also sometimes follow the business of carpenters and tailors. Lohárs sometimes become goldsmiths, and tailors follow the occupation of carpenters. The Brahma Kshatris, a very influential class of officials, are to be found in Júnágadh, as well as

Nágars and other Bráhmans of the Audich, Sompará, Sárasvata, Girnára, Patiálá, Gadhiá, and other tribes. There are many Khárwás, a class of seamen in the coast villages, both Hindús and Músalmáns in religion, and the coast Kolis also are some of them sailors.

There are many influential Muhammadan merchants in the towns of Júnágadh, Veráwal, Kútiáná, Wanthali, &c., both Khojás, Mehmans, Vohorás, and Arabs. The most intellectual class is that of the Nágars, who are the foremost officials of the State, although the Músalmáns also are employed in many high appointments. Salt is manufactured by Goláránás and Kolis. The Músalmáns in Júnágadh are officials, sipáhis, merchants, retail traders, grocers, carpet weavers, oil-pressers, bookbinders, and cutlers. The Pársis are principally ship agents or State servants.

Mode of living.

The Júnágadh population may, as to their mode of living, be divided into four classes. The mode of living of the upper class No. 1 may be thus described. Their cooking vessels and eating utensils, &c. are made of copper, brass, and silver. They keep a paid cook as a servant, and their women do not cook. Their food is wheat, rice, ghi, milk, sugar, fruit, &c. Their houses are their own property, and they keep carriages and horses and cattle of their own and probably own some land and gardens. Their women dress in silk with gold embroidery and wear handsome jewels. The men wear the finer cotton fabrics and turbans of silk or silk and cotton mixed. The 2nd class have their cooking vessels and eating utensils of brass and copper only, their women cook their food and wear less expensive ornaments. Their food is the same, and their houses though not so large are generally their own property, but they keep occasionally a horse and a cow or buffalo, and some of them may own a small patch of garden land. Their women dress in cotton fabrics and the men in the same material but of a coarser quality than class No. 1.

The 3rd class have copper and earthen cooking and eating vessels. Their wives cook and also collect firewood and cowdung, and spin and grind corn and also perform labour for hire. Their food is bájri and jowár bread and vegetables. They hire their houses and own neither land nor gardens. Both men and women wear the coarser cotton fabrics and coarse turbans or scarves loosely bound round the head. The women as a rule wear silver ornaments. The 4th class live in huts or under trees. Their wives cook and perform all kinds of labour and menial offices. Their food is jowár, and many of them combine begging with labour. They wear little clothing and that usually ragged and of the coarsest description, and the women wear ornaments of brass or copper. Some of the men wear caps or scarves.

Language.

Gújaráti is spoken by the entire population, but some of the Muhammadans speak Úrdú, Kachhi, or Sindhi. A few of the Makráni settlers speak the Makráni dialect. The Káthis speak a slightly different dialect of Gújaráti.

Houses.

The census returns of 1881 show in that year a total of 106,262 houses in the State, or an average of 32·36 to the square mile. Of these 24,668 were built of stone, brick, and mortar; the rest had walls of stone cemented with mud and with an outside plaster of mortar and roofs of thatch or tiles or were built with mud walls and roofs as above. Dwellings of the better sort lodged 175,184 persons, or 45·208 per cent. of the entire population at the rate of about 7·101 souls to each house. The 81,594 houses of the inferior sort, contained 212,315 or 54·791 per cent. of the entire population at the rate of 2·602 souls to a house.

Number of villages.

The State consists of 857 villages (including hamlets; of these 335 have a population of less than 200 inhabitants, 330 have from 200 to 500, 129 from 500 to 1,000, 47 from 1,000 to 2,000, 8 from 2,000 to 3,000, 1 from 3,000 to 5,000, 4 from 5,000 to 10,000, 2 from 10,000 to 15,000, and one (the Capital) from 20,000 to 30,000.

CHAPTER II.

TRADE.

Principal ports.

The principal ports in Júnágadh territory are those of (1) Veráwal, (2) Bheráí, (3) Nawá Bandar (the port of Uná-Delwárá), (4) Dhárá or Wahi Bandar, (5) Chorwár, (6) Sil, and (7) Mángrol. There are also roadsteads of Sutrápárá, Cháchurá, Belá, Hirákot, Simar, Rájpurá, Káliá Dhroh, and Dhámlej. Of the ports, Veráwal is by far the most important, and may be broadly said to supply grain, timber, and other necessaries to the greater part of Sorath and to the southern portion of Káthiáwár proper. Veráwal, properly speaking, is in its present state no harbour at all, but an open roadstead, and during the close season and rains, vessels are either hauled up upon the shore, or sent to Div, Jáfarábád, and other convenient harbours. The anchorage is not very good as there is much rock near the land. In 1866 Mr. Balliol Scott, C.E., was employed by the Júnágadh Darbár on harbour improvements. This gentleman reclaimed a portion of the shore and built a seawall, whereby the encroachments of the sea on the land in the rainy season were effectually prevented, But the advantage to be gained by prolonging the masonry pier, &c., were not appreciated by the Darbár, and the works were stopped in 1871. At present the pier is but 1,646 feet long and 11 feet high; a light-house 48 feet high stands on the end of it. Steamers cannot approach nearer than one mile from this pier, and the local authorities maintain that since its construction no advantage whatever has been derived, except that small coasting vessels when in its lee are in some degree sheltered from the violence of the waves, but that as large vessels cannot approach it, it is of no appreciable use. Looking at the few natural advantages of Veráwal as a port, it seems not unreasonable to believe that to make it even a second or third class harbour would involve an expense totally incommensurate with the advantages to be derived from increased trade, &c. The principal reason of the comparative prosperity of Veráwal is to be found in the large and wealthy trading population, causing it thus to be an important market. This population has been attracted there from ancient times—(1) when Veráwal was important as the port of Somnáth Pátan; (2) when, in the Muhammadan period, it was the point of departure for pilgrims to Makkáh, an advantage wrested from it or at all events largely shared in latter days by Surat; (3) in modern times the Bábi rulers of Júnágadh thus finding Veráwal by far the most important of their ports have bestowed on it more attention, and its vicinity to the town of Pátan and its position on the seaboard between Bombay and Karáchi have also been in its favour. Veráwal is now connected with Júnágadh by a fairly good made-road, and its trade may probably increase to a moderate extent, but it can never be a first-rate harbour. Steamers, however, beween Bombay and Karáchi constantly stop here in the open season, and the B. I. S. N. Company's Mail steamer plying between Bombay and Karáchi touches here both going and coming once a week. Veráwal generally imports grain from Karáchi and Bombay; piece-goods, groceries, iron manufactures, saltpetre, ivory, paper, gold and silver, from Bombay, to which place it exports cotton, wool, ghi, hides, horns, the leaves and bark of the Áwal (*cassia auriculata*) as well as the celebrated Veráwal onions. Vessels usually go to Karáchi in ballast, but sometimes molasses (gol) are exported. Timber and bamboos are imported from Daman and the Malabár Coast, whither grain is sometimes sent. Wheat is imported from Basrah in the Persian Gulf; and dates and dried fruits, &c., from Maskat. Cotton-seed and tobacco are imported from Bharúch and rice from Bhimri near Bombay. The population of Veráwal by the census of 1881 was 12,111 souls.

Bherái, the second port of importance in the Júnágadh State, is situated on a winding creek not inappropriately called Dúkhden (trouble giver). This creek joins the Deorápuri creek which in its turn falls into the creek called Motá Pát within a short distance from the sea. Bherái lies on the Júnágadh Bháwnagar frontier and is exposed to some competition from the ports of Máhuwá and Kathiwadar belonging to the latter State. On this account as well as its convenient position it has met with more attention than other minor ports of this State. The Bherái quay has been recently connected with the Devrápurí creek by a straight channel excavated in the mud and called the Súkhden (or ease giver). It however silts up very fast and requires a dredger to keep it clear and in good order. This channel is nearly a mile long by about 60 feet broad at the bottom of the channel, widening to 100 feet at the top. Bherái supplies grain to Bábriáwár and Dhári and Amreli and exports cotton from thence. The population of Bheraí was 1,171 souls by the census of 1881.

Nawábandar. Dhárábandar. Rájpúrá.

Nawábandar, situated on the southern coast not far from the Portuguese settlement of Diu, might be made into a very good harbour at a moderate expense, and as it is the port of the two fairly flourishing towns of Uná and Delwárá its trade might be no doubt developed, to at all events a moderate extent. But hitherto it has received little or no notice, the Darbár having bestowed all their attention on Veráwal and Bherái. Not far from Nawábandar to the eastward lies Dhárábandar which as well as Rájpúrá is capable of much improvement. These two ports, however, are cut off (by the Gir forest) from the inland country, and consequently cannot be expected to trade more than is needed for local requirements. The chief disadvantages at Nawábandar are rocks at the entrance of the harbour, and the want of a good pier. Judicious blasting would probably remove the rocks, and as stone abounds a good pier might be constructed at a moderate cost.

Chorwár and Sil.

Chorwár though classed among the ports is really only a roadstead and does little or no trade beyond local wants, the inland import trade being centered at Veráwal. Sil has greater capabilities, as there is a good creek, but there is no market, and much rock would have to be removed from the mouth of the creek ere vessels of any size could enter it with safety. At present it does little trade.

Mángrol. Mángrol, originally called Mangalpur Pátan, which (by dropping the p) was always called by the Persian historians Mangalúr or Mángálor, and by a common local custom (which pronounces Pálitáná as Pánitálá) is usually known at the present day as Mángrol. A fair amount of trade is done here; not so much owing to any natural advantages, which are of a most meagre kind, but to the presence of the Shekh of Mángrol and a large trading population. Mángrol was the head-quarters of the manufacture of inlaid ivory work and carved sandalwood, usually known as Bombay work. Mángrol also trades with the Red Sea and Persian Gulf as well as with Bombay, Karáchi, and other Gujarát ports. Mángrol is supposed by Colonel Yule and others to have been the Monoglossum of Ptolemy.

Júnágadh trade has not been at all disturbed by the B. B. and C. I. Railway branch to Wadhwán. The grain and ghi export trade (judging from sea exports and imports) has on the whole declined, and the import of grain increased. The cotton exports are a little over four times what they were in 1849-50. Of this no doubt a considerable proportion is imported from neighbouring tálukás, but it shows nevertheless an increased area under cotton. During the seasons of 1877, and 1878 however, owing first to insufficient and then to excessive rain, but little cotton was grown in the country. Hence, while grain imports had, owing to the scarcity, increased, the export of cotton temporarily sensibly diminished. Sugar stuffs (excepting molasses) have been imported in increasing quantities, while the export of molasses has (owing to increasing cultivation of sugarcane) been yearly (fluctuations apart) on a larger scale. The export of wool has, on the whole, improved, but the trade in this article is insignificant. Oil, oil-seeds, and metal are now imported in larger quantities, but the trade in ivory seems stationary, as though the value of the import shown is greater, the price has proportionately risen. Piece-goods alone amongst imports (if grain be excepted) shows a marked rise, while the entire collapse of the sea-exports trade in these goods points to the decline in native manufacture noticed in the Nawánagar Trade Returns.

On the whole, trade may be expected to increase when the waste lands, so abundant in this State, come under the plough, and when public works receive more attention. The cotton export trade will probably sooner or later swallow up the grain export trade, and the grain import trade may be expected to increase.

The accompanying Trade Return will explain in detail the amounts actually exported and imported of each separate article. More reliance may be placed on the figures of the sea exports and imports than on those of the land.

Shipping.

The following return will show the number of vessels which sailed from and visited the Júnágadh ports during the year 1876-77. From this it appears that 1,191 vessels arrived at and 864 quitted the Júnágadh ports during that year:—

Statement showing the number and tonnage of the vessels trading to Júnágadh ports in 1876-77.

No.	Ports.	Vessels arrived at Júnágadh ports.			Vessels departed from Júnágadh ports.			Remarks.
		Number.	Tonnage.	Average size in Tons.	Number.	Tonnage.	Average size in Tons.	
1	Kachh ports	13	47	3⅗	39	291	7½	
16	Káthiáwár ports	395	2,932	7⅞	125	899	7⅕	
2	Portuguese ports	26	196	7½	8	9	1⅛	
5	Gujarát ports...........	71	2,370	33⅖	12	189	15¾	
1	Bombay	326	6,399	19⅗	571	11,549	20$\frac{4}{19}$	
14	Konkan ports...........	183	3,586	19⅗	89	3,807	42$\frac{69}{89}$	
2	Karáchi and Kheti, &c.	95	2,410	...	18	257	14$\frac{5}{18}$	
2	Persian Gulf	81	2,423	36$\frac{1}{16}$	2	18	9	
1	Aden	1	26	26	...	...	...	
		1,191	20,389	...	864	17,019	...	

These vessels are mostly coasting craft, but include several steamers.

The trade with all ports except Bombay and Karáchi is stationary if not diminishing; but the trade with the two ports mentioned is largely on the increase.

Course of trade.

Salt Manufacture.

The revenue realized from salt manufactured in the Júnágadh State for 1876-77 amounted in all to Rupees 19,165. The names of the principal salt works are (1) Bherái, (2) Kaḍiáli, (3) Ningálá, (4) Sejaliá, (5) Dhámlej, (6) Veráwal, (7) Mahiári, (8) Nágasri (disputed with Jáfarábád). The salt manufactured is of the kind called ghásiá, and the works of Dhámlej and Bherái are the best; the salt work of Dhámlej is probably the most ancient in the province. So much are the Dhámlej salt works renowned in Sorath and Káthiáwár proper, that a foolish person is, in local parlance, said to be *Dhámlej no kácho,* or ignorant of Dhámlej (without salt or wit). The salt is manufactured by a tribe of Kolis called Ágriás, and is inferior to the Wadágrá salt of Khárághorá.

Salt and Salt works.

About 3,10,000 Bengál maunds of this salt are manufactured annually, of which about 1,25,000 maunds are consumed in Júnágadh territory; the remainder is sold in Káthiáwár proper, Amreli, and other neighbouring tálúkáhs.

Amount annually produced.

The Darbár pays the Ágriás for their labour and sells the salt to local and foreign merchants, and derives therefrom about Rs. 20,000 per annum. Much attention is now given to salt manufacture and to the sale and storing the same. Formerly it was sold by the Ágriás, who used to receive as remuneration a portion of the salt produced. This they sold as they best could.

Share of revenue accruing to Darbar.

Money lending.

The principal moneylenders in the Júnágadh State are Wániás, Nágars, Bráhmans, Bramhkshatris, Lohánás, Bhátiás, Kunbis, Vohrás, Khojás, Mehmans, and other Muhammadans; among merchants the usual rate of interest is from 3 to 4 per cent. among cultivators and grásiás from 7 to 12 per cent. The rate of interest is lowered proportionally, if land or jewels be pledged as security for payment.

Banking.

It is customary to present a banker with a small sum when borrowing money from him, such sum is called manotiáman or kothli chorámau, watio, or other local name, and so when a loan is repaid, it is usual for the creditor to remit a portion of the interest.

Kori coinage.

The current coin in the Júnágadh State is the kori called Diwánshái. A mint was established in Júnágadh subsequent to the conquest of the province by the Moghal Government to coin mahmúdis, which formerly were current in this country, and which are now represented by the modern kori; but this mint was closed during the disturbances which marked the dissolution of the Imperial power in Gujarát. It was also closed for a short time during the reign of the Emperor Sháh Jahán on the representation of the provincial Diwán Muhammad Sábar. The mint was re-opened by the celebrated Diwán Amarji in about A. D. 1780 in the reign of Nawáb Sáhib Hámid Khán. These kories were called after the Diwán Amarji, Diwánsháis. But others say, with perhaps greater probability, that they are called Diwansháis after the Nawáb's title of Diwán. The average exchange value of the Diwánshái kori as compared with the imperial rupee is as 3½ to 1, but this value fluctuates considerably. At the present moment a rupee is worth a little less than 3½ koris.

This kori at present consists of 12 wáls of metal in the following proportions:—7½ wáls silver and 4½ wáls copper; a half kori is also coined.

Gold coins.

A few gold kories were coined as experiment in A. D. 1876, but they soon fell out of circulation and are now no longer coined.

The following copper coins are coined and in current use in the Júnágadh State,—(1) half dokrás, of which two go to the dokrá; (2) dokras, of which 40 go to the kori. Portuguese riáls are current in Uná, Bábriáwár, and the Sonth. The average value of the riál is 8 Diwánshái koris, but they are of several kinds.

The accompanying table will show the rise in the cost of agricultural produce during the last forty or fifty years:—

Price Statement.

Name of Produce.	1831-32. Number of lbs. sold for one rupee (two shillings).	1858-59. Number of lbs. sold for one rupee (two shillings).	1878-79. Number of lbs. sold for one rupee (two shillings)
Millet (bájri)	92	56	18½
Jowár (*holcus sorghum*)	84	72	20¼
Wheat	56	50	14¾
Gram	92	50	20¼
Rice	33½	20	14¾
Pulse (dál)	52	48	16½
Cotton (cleaned)	6	6	5¼
Tobacco	2¾	4½	4¼
Ghi	5	4	1¾

The rise in the price of both skilled and unskilled labour is shown in the following statement. The rise commenced about the same time as the rise in the price of cotton consequent on the American war in 1863:—

Table of Wages.

Classes of labourers.	Daily wages in 1833-34.	Daily wages in 1858-59.	Daily wages in 1875-76.
	Annas.	Annas.	Annas.
Masons	4½	5½	11¼
Sawyers	3⅓	4½	9
Bricklayers	2⅔	3½	5½
Carpenters	3⅓	4½	9
Labourers	2½	3⅓	5½
Tailors	4½	5½	9

Weights and measures.

The principal weights and measures in use in Júnágadh territory are as follows :—

Weights in the town of Júnágadh.

80 Tolás (or Imperial Rupees). = 1 Sir.
16 Sirs.............................. = 1 Maund.
5 Maunds .... = 1 Kothlo.
4 Kothlás .... = 1 Khándi.

Weights used in the Júnágadh Districts.

22 Imperial Rupees (or tolás). = 1 Sir.
40 Sirs.............................. = 1 Maund.

But sugarcandy, betelnut, and dried fruits are sold by a maund consisting of 20 sirs Júnágadh town weight.

Goldsmiths' weights.

1½ Rice grains .... = 1 Mag.
16 Mags .... = 1 Chanoti.
8 Chanotis .... = 1 Wál.
16 Wáls .... = 1 Gadiáná.
1¼ Gadiánás .... = 1 Tolá or Imperial Rupee.

Grain measures.

2 Gadiás .... = 1 Pawálá (or measure of 20 tolás).
2 Pawálás ... ... = 1 Adhwáli.
2 Adhwális .... = 1 Páli.
5 Pális .... = 1 Máp.
4 Máps .... = 1 Shái.
8 Sháis .... = 1 Háro.
2 Háros .... = 1 Kalshi (or khándi).

Cotton weight.

44 Dokrás.................. = 1 Sir.
45 Sirs .... = 1 Maund.
2 Maunds .... = 1 Tolú.
20 Tolús .... = 1 Bhár.

Milk measure.

18	Tolás	=	1 Pali.
2½	Palis	=	1 Tabúri.
4	Tabúris	=	1 Sir.
40	Sirs	=	1 Maund.

Pearl weights.

16	Badáms (almonds) .	=	1 Dokra.
100	Dokrás	=	1 Chav.
6¾	Chavs	=	1 Taká.
13¼	Takás	=	1 Rati.
24	Ratis	=	1 Tánk.

CHAPTER III.

HISTORY.

The founder of the Bábi family was one Bahádúr Khán, a native of Afghánistán, who appears to have risen to distinction in the reign of the Emperor Sháh Jahán, who sent one of his sons, Sher Khán Bábi, in company with prince Morád Bakhsh, when that prince took up the viceroyalty of Gújarát in about A. D. 1654, and in 1663-64 Sher Khán, who was a man of great ability and firmness, was appointed thánahdár of the Chúnwál, a district requiring much ability to keep under control, as it abounded in daring and rebellious kolis. Sher Khán had four sons, viz. (1) Muhammad Mûbáriz Khán, who afterwards, about A. D. 1674, was in charge of one of the posts under Kaḍi; while his brother (2) Muhammad Múzafar was governor of the Kaḍ district; (3) Jáfar Khán, whose descendants founded the three great Bábi houses of Gújarát, viz. (1) Rádhanpúr, (2) Júnágadh, and (3) Wáḍásinor, commonly called Bálásinor; and (4) Sháhbáz Khán now represented by the Ránpúr house under Júnágadh. Jáfar Khán succeeded his father in about A. D. 1690, and shortly afterwards, for services rendered in Gújarát, received the title of Safdar Khán and was appointed deputy governor of Pátan. In 1694 his brother, Muhammad Múbáriz, was appointed deputy governor of Waḍnagar. Muhammad Múbáriz now appears to have relieved his brother at Pátan, but was shortly after killed while chastising the kolis of Sámprah; he was succeeded by Safdar Khán, and his son, Muhammad Ázam, &c., received suitable appointments. In 1698, however, a difference arose between the viceroy of Gújarát Shújáat Khán and Safdar Khán, and Safdar Khán resigned his office in disgust and retired to Málwá, whence he did not return until after the expiration of Shújáat Khán's viceroyalty. But in

Bahádúr Khán, about A. D. 1630-1654.

Sher Khán, A. D. 1654-1690.

Jáfar Khán, otherwise called Safdar Khán, A. D. 1690-1725.

about 1703 A. D., when Dúrgádás Ráthor was again disturbing the peace of the country, Safdar Khán volunteered to kill or capture him, and drove him from the province and nearly succeeded in capturing him, and was again employed under the viceroy in Gújarát, and in about 1704 was appointed to the command of the district of Bijápur, which lies to the north of Áhmadábád.

In about 1705 Safdar Khán Bábi was sent with Nazar Ali Khán and an army to oppose the Maráthás who had now for the first time entered and laid waste the southern districts. Unfortunately, however, a great jealousy existed betwixt Safdar Khán and Nazar Ali Khán and their counsels were not unanimous. While encamped at Ratanpur (now in Rájpiplá territory) they were suddenly attacked by the Maráthás under Dhanáji Jádao and completely routed, and Safdar Khán was himself taken prisoner and his son slain. Shortly afterwards the main body of the imperial army under Abdúl Hámid Khán, who was then in charge of the province, was defeated by the Maráthás, and Abdúl Hamid and many other nobles were taken prisoners. Two sons of Safdar Khán, viz., Salábat Muhammad and Muhammad Sher, who were with Abdúl Hamid Khán, cut their way through the Maráthá hosts and escaped. A heavy ransom was extorted by the victorious southrons ere their prisoners were released. Shortly after Safdar Khán's return Dúrgádás Ráthor again rebelled. Safdar Khán in about A. D. 1706 offered to kill or capture him on condition that he should, if successful, be made governor of Pátan. As Safdar Khán was about this time made governor of this district and as we hear no more of Dúrgádás from this date it seems probable that Safdar Khán succeeded in killing him. From this date Safdar Khán was perhaps the most prominent of the local nobility, and his numerous sons received important appointments, thus we hear of his son Khán Jahán receiving the title of Jawán Mard Khán and being appointed in about 1716 to the charge of Rádhanpúr. Another son, Salábat Muhammad Khán, was at this time deputy in Gohilwár, where he did good service during the dissensions between the viceroy Mahárájá Ajitsingh and the celebrated Haidar Kúli Khán, who was then in the semi-independent charge of Súrat and Kambay. Afterwards an affray occurred between Haidar Kúli Khán's troops and those of Safdar Khán and his relatives, owing to some trifling dispute about a water-carrier, and the Bábis were forced to take refuge at Pálanpur; but afterwards, through the mediation of Muhammad Firoz Jálori of Pálanpur, a reconciliation between them and Haidar was effected, and Safdar Khán was appointed deputy governor of Godhrá. At this time his son Salábat Muhammad Khán appears to have been governor of Viramgaum, and Jawán Mard Khán governor of Rádhanpur, while a son of Salábat Khán's, named Muhammad Bahádur, was foujdár of the districts immediately around Áhmadábád and afterwards was appointed in about A. D. 1722 to the charge of Sádrá and Virpur in the Mahi Kánthá with the title of Sher Khán. Haidar Kûli Khán, one of the leading men of the time, was in passes through its lands. It is about nine miles south-east of Kúndlá. The name is said to be derived from Gátra (body) and Gadá to bury, because Báwá Somnáth of Gorakhmadi buried himself alive here. The Káthis of Gádhakdá had carried off his cattle. The Báwá accordingly went to Gádhakdá and demanded their restoration, but the Káthis refused. After waiting for three or four days fasting he dug a grave and descended therein. On seeing this the Káthis remonstrated with him and offered to come to terms, but he replied, "When an ascetic has once entered the grave, he may not return." Then he cursed the Káthis and said that they would never be prosperous in future, and then caused himself to be buried alive under a banyán tree still called Somnáth no Wad. Chomlá Khumán of Gádhakdá distinguished himself by recovering some cattle of Júnágadh villages from the Khasiás of the Bhávnagar village of Sedardá. The population but he was no match for Nizám-úl-Múlk, one of the first of whose measures was to appoint Safdar Khán Bábi as his deputy. The Bábis who had never quite forgiven Haidar's first warfare against them, and who somewhat feared that should he attain to supreme power in the province he might despoil them of their estates, at once ranged themselves on the side of order and the Nizám, and their example, added to the general distrust felt for Haidar, caused most of the local Muhammadan nobility to follow the same course, and Haidar was forced to forego opposition and retire from the province. The Nizám shortly afterwards visited Gújarát, but after placing his uncle Hámid Khán in authority as his deputy, he too returned to the capital. The Bábis, as was natural, increased in power and importance and were rewarded for their conduct in supporting the Nizám. More troublous times were however at hand. In about A. D. 1723 Múbáriz-úl-Múlk Sarbúland Khán Bahádúr was appointed viceroy and he appointed Shújáat Khan to act as his deputy. The Nizám's uncle and deputy Hámid Khán, however, was determined to oppose him by force of arms, and was only dissuaded from open resistance by the united counsels of Safdar Khán Bábi and his sons Salábat Khán and Jawán Mard Khán. He accordingly withdrew to Dohad on the frontier of Málwá and thence watched his opportunity while Shújáat Khán entered the capital and assumed office. Hámid Khán now invoked the aid of the Maráthás and finally defeated and killed Shújáat Khan, and regained possession of Áhmadábád, and also slew Rústam Ali Khán, the governor of Súrat and brother to Shújáat Khán, but was obliged in return for their assistance to grant the chouth to the north of the Mahi river, to Kantáji Kadam, one of the Maráthá leaders, and the chouth to the south of that river to Piláji Gáekwár. During these internal disturbances the Bábis steadily consolidated their power, and their alliance became a matter of the first importance to the contending parties. Hámid Khán's usurpation caused great consternation at Delhi, and Sarbuland Khán, in about A.D. 1725, at the head of a large army, marched upon Gújarát to expel him. Jawán Mard Khán Bábi joined Sarbuland Khán, and at this juncture Safdar Khán died.

Salábat Muhammad Khán, A. D. 1725-1730.

At the time of the arrival of Sarbuland Khán in the province Salábat Muhammad Khán had for some reason or other been removed from his charge of Viramgaum, but Sarbuland Khán at once reinstated him, while he appointed Jawán Mard Khán to be governor of Pátan. Salábat Muhammad Khán from his long tenure of office at Viramgaum, coupled with the fact that he enjoyed the jágir of Goghá, caused him to have great influence within the peninsula of Káthiáwár, and this influence he much increased both by intervening in the internal dissensions of the province and by mediating betwixt the chiefs and the viceroy during múlkgiri expeditions. His influence and co-operation at this period was particularly essential to the foujdár of Júnágadh, whose power during the anarchy and internal dissensions of the time was rapidly declining. As an instance of his influence, I may here fitly notice that Jám Tamáchi of Nawánagar was seated on the gádi principally through his aid, and the Ráj of Halwad caused one of his kinsmen to give him a daughter in marriage to win him to the cause. After Jám Tamáchi was enthroned, Salábat Muhammad Khán received in return for his services the three villages of Trákurá, Charakhḍi, and Dahiyá, afterwards sold to Kumbhoji of Gonḍal by his sons Dilerkhán and Sher Zamán Khán, the future founders of the tálukah of Bántwá, and these villages belong to Gondal to this day. In about 1728-29 Asad Ali Khán, foujdár of Júnágadh, died, and on his deathbed nominated Salábat Muhammad Khán as deputy governor of that fortress. Salábat Muhammad Khán, however, whose position at Viramgaum was most important, preferred to send his son Sher Khán, who was both brave and able, as his deputy, and though shortly after the Emperor appointed Ghulám Muhyaúd-din, son of the deceased Asad Ali, as his successor in the permanent appointment, that officer found it advisable to continue Sher Khán as his deputy. The Maráthás now commenced to extend their ravages to Sorath, and Sher Khán Bábi made himself so useful, that although Asad Ali Khán afterwards nominated another deputy in his place, nevertheless through the viceroy's influence Sher Khán was confirmed.

In about 1729 Jawán Mard Khán was killed while chastising the excesses of the kolis of Bálor, a village in his government. Bálor was laid waste in revenge for his death, and at the request of Salábat Muhammad Khán, his eldest son, Kamálúd-din Khán, received the title of Jawán Mard Khán borne by his father, and with it the estates of Sami and Múnjpúr, while his second son Muhammad Anwar Khán received the title of Safdar

Khán and the foujdári of Rádhanpúr. In about the year 1730 Udikaran, Desái of Viramgaum, was murdered by a Kasbáti of that town named Ali Táuk and Salábat Muhammad Khán was proceeding to investigate the matter, when he was taken ill and died at a village named Páldi.

Sher Khán, who on becoming independent assumed the title of Bahádúr Khán, A.D. 1730-1758.

Early in A.D. 1730 Mir Ismail, deputy of Ghúlám Mahyá-úd-din Khán, arrived at Júnágadh and took charge of the foujdári from Sher Khán Bábi, who retired in disgust to his jágir of Goghá. In this year, however, the viceroy Múbáriz-úl-Mulk was superseded after some fighting by the Máhárájá Abhyesingh, who had been joined by Jáwan Mard Khán Bábi and his brother Safdar Khán. When the Máhárájá reached Áhmadábád, Sher Khán repaired thither, and presented him with an elephant and was confirmed in his ancestral possessions. In 1732 the viceroy alarmed at the successes of Piláji Gáekwár, who had conquered Baroda and Dabhoi, procured that leader's assassination at Dákor and shortly afterwards recovered Baroda, which city and district he placed under the government of Sher Khán Bábi as foujdár. In 1733 Umábái, widow of Khanderáo Senápati, whose servant Piláji was, marched at the head of an army on Áhmadábád to avenge his loss. Eventually, however, peace was concluded between her and the Máhárájá and she withdrew by way of Baroda. Here Sher Khán drew out his forces to oppose her passage and only suffered her to depart without giving battle, on her satisfying him that she had concluded a treaty with the viceroy. During Sher Khán's absence at Baroda, Búrhán-úl-Múlk, the most powerful noble of the Court of Delhi, obtained the grant of the jágir of Goghá for his protege Sohráb Khán, an ex-governor of Súrat, in spite of the viceroy's confirmation of that jágir to Sher Khán. Sher Khán's younger brethren who were in Goghá resisted, but were compelled to quit that town, and when the náib foujdár of Júnágadh complained of Sohráb Khán's appointment, Búrhán-úl-Múlk managed to obtain for himself the appointment of foujdár of Sorath, to which he at once appointed Sohráb Khán as his deputy.

Now Sher Khán besides Goghá had the ancestral jágir of Bálásinor (Wáḍásinor) in Gújarát, and in 1734 he went on a visit thither, leaving Muhammad Sarbáz in command at Baroda. This opportunity was too good to be neglected by the Maráthás, and Máhádáji Gáekwár (brother of Piláji) who then held Jambúsar, wrote secretly to Songadh to Dámáji for aid and at once marched on Baroda, but the garrison refused to surrender. Sher Khán at once set out to relieve the town, but Máhádáji leaving a sufficient force to continue the investment of the place marched to meet him. After a stubborn conflict Sher Khán was defeated, and forced to retire to Bálásinor, while Máhádáji Gáekwár returned triumphant to prosecute the siege. The garrison now hopeless of succour surrendered, and since that day Baroda has been the head-quarters of the Gáekwár family. Sher Khán now went to Áhmadábád, where from his gallant conduct and tried ability as well as from his family influence, he was high in favour with the deputy viceroy, and shortly afterwards was appointed to the important foujdári of Viramgaum (so long held by his father) in place of his cousin Jawán Mard Khán, who had made himself unpopular owing to his harshness to the Desái family of that town. In 1735 Sohráb Khán, foujdár of Júnágadh, was killed in battle fighting with Ratansingh Bhandári, deputy viceroy, at Dholi near Dhandhúká, and Mohsan Khán Khálvi was appointed to his office. At this time, Dámáji Gáekwár through the treachery of Bhávsingh Desái, managed to obtain possession of Viramgaum, and aware of the importance of the post, he left Rangoji there in great strength and returned to Gújarát. The foujdár of Viramgaum, especially during Salábat Khán Bábi's long tenure of the office, united the ordinary duties of military governor and that of lord marcher, and he usually accompanied the múlkgiri forces, or was sent on in advance to settle the tribute amicably. Hence on this account and that if the holder of Viramgaum were hostile, it would be difficult for the múlkgiri forces to enter the peninsula, there was understood to be attached to this office a kind of right to collect the tribute of the peninsula. Of this right the Maráthás were not slow to avail themselves, and shortly after this conquest they commenced their first collections, though the right to collect was by no means surrendered by the imperial viceroy, who also when he found an opportunity made múlkgiri expeditions into Sorath. This occupation of Viramgaum, however, by the Maráthás severed in a great measure the connection between the provincial viceroy and the Sorath foujdár, who was obliged to depend more on his own resources to prevent the Maráthás encroaching, by collecting tribute from chieftains properly subordinate to him. At the same time in order to check the Maráthá aggression, it became a matter of primary importance to the viceroy to have an efficient foujdár at Júnágadh, even though the share of the imperial tribute collected by such foujdár were applied to his own uses, as anything was preferable to Maráthá aggrandizement.

After the conquest of Viramgaum, Sher Khán Bábi went to reside with his relations at Kheḍá, thence visiting his jágir of Bálásinor as often as he found convenient.

In about 1736 Sher Khán Bábi came to Áhmadábád where Ratansingh Bhandári, the deputy of the Máhárájá Abhyesingh, entertained him most favourably, and shortly afterwards gave him an appointment at Pitlád, where he had some differences with Momin Khán.

In about 1737 Momin Khán was appointed viceroy, but as he was unable to take up the appointment without the assistance of the local nobility, he induced Jawán Mard Khán Bábi to join him by promising him the government of Pátan, which however Pahár Khán Jálori refused to surrender. Momin Khán, however, now proceeded to the capital and publicly assumed office. Sher Khán knowing that Momin Khán was not well disposed towards him, now withdrew to his jágir of Bálásinor, while Ratansingh Bhandári prepared to defend Áhmadábád. In this year the foujdári of Júnágadh was conferred on Mir Hazabar Ali Khán in place of Mohsan Khán.

Momin Khán now despairing of obtaining possession of Áhmadábád by peaceable means, made overtures to the Maráthás, and agreed, should they succeed in expelling the Márwáḍis, to grant them half of the revenues of Gújarat, the city of Áhmadábád, its adjacent lands, and the port of Kambay, being alone excepted. The Maráthás under Rangoji now joined him as did Jawán Mard Khán Bábi, and thus reinforced he advanced and laid siege to the capital. In the meantime the Máhárájá Abbyesingh, who was with the emperor, was so incensed at his supersession by Momin Khán that he threatened rebellion, and the courtiers anxious at any cost to avert his wrath, persuaded the emperor to again appoint him viceroy of Gújarát. This was done, but secret instructions were sent to Momin Khán to expel his partizans if he were able to do so, and accordingly Momin Khán pressed the siege of Áhmadabad. Finally in about A.D. 1738 Momin Khán compelled Ratansingh Bhandári to quit the capital, which he entered with the Maráthás. During this time of anarchy the Maráthas had availed themselves of their commanding position at Viramgaum to make several expeditions into the peninsula to levy tribute, and the foujdár Hazabar Ali Khán had been able to do but little towards checking them.

Momin Khán now governed the city jointly with the Maráthás and rewarded Jawán Mard Khán Bábi by granting him the promised government of Pátan, while on his younger brother, Zoráwar Khán Bábi, he conferred the charge of the parganah of Kherálú. The emperor, who was just then anxious to humble the Ráthors of Jodhpúr, was so delighted at their expulsion, that he sent Momin Khán a sword, a dress of honour, and other valuable articles. Sher Khán seeing that it would no longer be politic to hold aloof, paid his respects to the viceroy in company with Jawán Mard Khán and shortly afterwards was appointed deputy foujdár of Sorath in place of Mir Dost Ali, deputy of Hazabar Ali Khán. Sher Khán, however, did not consider it advisable to proceed to Sorath until he should have further ingratiated himself with Momin Khán, whom accordingly he accompanied on a mûlkgiri expedition to North Gújarát. At this juncture Mámú Khán, who had been appointed as his deputy in Sorath by Hazabar Ali Khán, arrived and complained to the viceroy regarding his nomination of Sher Khán. Momin Khán put him off by saying that as neither had hitherto assumed charge of their duties, he would make a reference to the emperor and meanwhile granting Sher Khán leave to visit his jágir at Goghá secretly directed him to proceed thence to Júnagádh to take up his appointment. Sher Khán accordingly at once proceeded thither and relieved Mir Dost Ali and took into his employ all that officer's troops and established himself so firmly that Mámú Khán found it advisable to withdraw his pretensious and retire. At this juncture Hazabar Ali Khán died and the emperor nominated in his stead Himat Ali Khán, nephew of Momin Khán, to the foujdári of Sorath, and Himat Ali wrote to his uncle to procure for him a fitting deputy. As the Maráthá incursions increased yearly and as Sher Khán Bábi was able to hold his own with them, Momin Khán confirmed him as deputy.

In the meantime the Maráthás continued their incursions into the peninsula with more or less success, and Rangoji established himself at Borsad, and thus the Maráthás could enter either by way of Viramgaum or Borsad. Sher Khán conducted the management of Sorath with much judgment, and while strengthening himself in Júnágadh and the immediate vicinity, yet contrived not to draw on himself the enmity of the Maráthás; and specially he contrived to conciliate Rangoji.

In 1743, Momin Khán died, and Fidá-úd-din Khán and Momin Khán's son Múftakhir Khán received an imperial order to carry on the government of Gújarát until a new viceroy should be appointed. Rangoji now conceived the idea of seizing on the government, and with this idea he invited Sher Khán to join him. Sher Khán who saw in this invitation a means of furthering his own ambition, at once proceeded to Borsad, and commenced plundering some of the Kambay villages. Rangoji offered Sher Khán the post of deputy viceroy should he be successful, and made some futile attempts to assassinate Fidá-úd-din Khán and Múftakhir Khán, but these nobles joining their forces marched against him, and succeeded in detaching Sher Khán from his alliance. Rangoji was now defeated and eventually agreed to surrender both Borsad and Viramgaum, Sher Khán becoming his security.

Sher Khán was now in a very powerful position, he had befriended Rangoji, who was unaware of his treachery, while he had no longer Maráthá incursions to dread from Viramgaum and Borsad, and as Fidá-úd-din Khán and Múftakhir Khán were by no means firmly established at Áhmadábád, he had not much to dread from them; however, with a view to seeing what he might be able to obtain as well as to see what was going on, he accompanied them to the capital. At this time, however, Dámáji Gáekwár at the head of a large army marched to Kambay. Sher Khán who saw the importance of standing well with the Maráthás, suffered Rangoji who was residing with him on parole to escape to Borsad, where he soon effected a junction with Dámáji and conjointly laid siege to Pitlád. In the meantime Fidá-úd-din Khán was extremely enraged with Sher Khán for suffering Rangoji to escape, and Sher Khán, deeming it unwise under such circumstances to remain longer at the capital, fled to his jágir at Bálásinor, whence he might watch events at his ease. Jawán Mard Khán Bábi, seeing the weakness of the viceroys, now by means of a forged order and a certain amount of force, contrived to usurp the control of Áhmadábád, and though about this time Múftakhir Khán received a formal appointment as viceroy from the emperor, he was unable to dispossess Jawán Mard Khán, and was compelled to leave the city and join Rangoji, and finally to withdraw to Kambay.

Khande Ráo Gáekwár, brother of Dámáji, now joining Rangoji, marched on Áhmadábád and demanded a restitution of their former rights. Jawán Mard Khán marched out to give them battle, and was joined by Sher Khán, but eventually Jawán Mard Khán thought it advisable to grant the Máráthás considerable concessions, and peace was concluded, after which Sher Khán returned to Bálásinor.

In 1744 Fakhr-úd-daulah was appointed viceroy. He nominated Jawán Mard Khán as his deputy, but after a few months set out to take up his appointment, and on his way passed through Bálásinor, where he was received by Sher Khán with much respect. Jawán Mard Khán determined to resist, and accordingly won over Sher Khán and Raisinghji of Idar to his side, and drew up in order of battle a few miles from the capital. At first Fakhr-ûd-daulah was successful, but Sher Khán's and Raisinghji's desertions balanced matters, and next day he was surrounded and taken prisoner by Safdar Khán Bábi, brother of Jawán Mard Khán.

Dissensions now commenced among the Máráthás, and Khande Ráo Gáckwár placed Rangoji in confinement at Borsad, and appointed Trimbak Ráo Pandit as his deputy in Áhmadábád in place of Moro Pandit. Rangoji, however, was speedily released by order of Umábái, and he proceeded to Áhmadábád and expelled Trimbak Ráo, and cemented afresh his alliance with Jawán Mard Khán.

Trimbak Ráo, Púnáji Vithal, and Fakhr-ûd-daulah, now seized on the districts to the chouth of which the Maráthás were entitled, Rangoji therefore besought aid of Sher Khán. Sher Khán agreed and commenced operations by plundering Mahúdhá and Nariád, and thence proceeded to Kapaḍwanj and advanced on the Maráthás alone. He however got the worst of some severe skirmishing, and only averted defeat by negotiation. In the meantime hearing of Rangoji's arrival at Bálásinor, Sher Khán managed that very night to withdraw to Kapaḍwanj, and though pursued by Púnáji and Fakhr-ûd-daulah, he contrived next day to effect a junction with Rangoji. Subsequently in a battle fought with Fakhr-ûd-daulah, Sher Khán was wounded, and he and Rangoji were forced to take shelter in Kapaḍwanj. Here, however, Rangoji by a payment of Rupees 2,00,000 obtained the assistance of Holkar, who was then on the Málwá frontier, and on hearing of his approach, Fakhr-ûd-daulah raised the siege of Kapaḍwanj.

In 1747, Sher Khán and Rájá Ráisinghji of Idar, appear to have joined Fakhr-ûd-daulah against Jawán Mard Khán Bábi, but were unsuccessful and obliged to retire from Áhmadábád, to which city they had laid siege; and in the same year they joined their old ally Rangoji in defending Borsad, against Dámáji and Khande Ráo Gáekwár, aided by a force from Jawán Mard Khán Bábi. Borsad however was taken after a siege of five months, and Sher Khán was obliged to return to Bálásinor and Ráisinghji to Idar.

Sher Khán had now made two powerful enemies, namely, Damáji Gáekwár and Jawán Mard Khán Bábi, he therefore deemed it advisable to retire to Júnágadh, where his wives, Láḍḍi Bibi and Aman Bibi, had been carrying on the management of affairs for him, and accordingly in about 1748, he placed his son Sardár Muhammad Khán at Bálásinor, and himself withdrew to Júnágadh.

In this year Kánoji Tákpar, a Maráthá leader, joining Fakhr-úd-daulah made a tribute-collecting expedition into Sorath, and besieged and took the town of Wanthali, distant about ten miles from Júnágadh, and desired to attack that city, but were compelled to retire without accomplishing their object.

Sher Khán now entirely withdrew from the affairs of Gújarát, and endeavoured to consolidate an independent rule at Júnágadh, and assumed the title of Bahádúr Khán, and the style of Nawáb. His assumption of this title had caused Colonel Walker (Government Selections No. XXXIX, new series, page 179, paragraph 37) to make some serious blunders, which he aggravates by mistaking Salábat Khán, Sher Khán's father, for his, Sher Khán's, son.

It seems that after Sher Khán had arranged affairs at Júnágadh on a firm basis, he once more visited Gújarát, but finding no adequate field there for his ambition, he returned to Júnágadh. During his absence a Purbiá named Wasant Rái got possession of the city of Júnágadh, but was expelled by Diwán Dalpatrám. After his expulsion, however, Wasant Rai joined Mánsiá Khánt, and they contrived to seize on the Úparkot, where they maintained themselves for some time by plundering the surrounding country, but eventually after an occupation of about thirteen months they were forced to quit that stronghold. Diwán Dalpatrám died in about 1750-51, and after this a Kámdár of his named Jaganáth Jhálá rose into importance, especially in virtue of his being vakil of the Arabs. The Arabs, however, to whom arrears of pay were due, became violent, and seized on the Úparkot. The Nawáb, who was unable to levy tribute or contributions save in the immediate vicinity, was unable to satisfy their demands, and accordingly had recourse to stratagem to expel them. He first persuaded Jaganáth Jhálá and his brother Rúdraji to join him, and then on pretence of a múlkgiri expedition, withdrew with his army from the city, taking Jaganáth Jhálá with him, as if with a view of making arrangements for the pay of the Arabs. While he was absent, Rúdraji persuaded the Arabs to remove all the ammunition and provision from the fort, saying that he would lay in a fresh stock. No sooner was it all removed, than he sent a secret messenger to the Nawáb, who at once returned to the city and laid siege to the fort, but without success. Finally, says the author of the Tárikh-i-Sorath, in 1754, Shekh Muhammad Zubaidi took a sum of money from Jáḍejá Kúmbhoji as the price of Dhoráji, and giving it to the Arabs, expelled them from the city. Nawáb Bahádúr Khán does not seem to have had any more internal dissensions to contend with, and established himself on an independent basis at Júnágadh, without interfering further in the affairs of Gújarát. He died in 1758, and was succeeded by his son Máhábat Khán, who was present in Júnágadh at the time of his father's death.

Nawáb Máhábat Khán, A. D. 1758-1775.

Nawáb Máhábat Khán was seated on the gádi by the nobles and chief men of Júnágadh, during the absence of his brother Sardár Muhammad Khán at Bálásinor, but his rule was speedily disturbed by intrigues.

Foremost among these was one set on foot by the Nawáb's aunt, Bibi Sáhibah Súltán, sister of the late Nawáb Bahádúr Khán. This lady had married Bahádúr Khán's cousin Shahámat Khán Bábi, son of Sher Khán, uncle to the late Nawáb, and had by him one son, Jáfar Khán (now deceased) who had left two sons, Múzafar Khán and Fatehyáb Khán. Súltán Bibi was anxious if possible to entirely set aside Máhábat Khán, and accordingly associating with her Jamádár Sulimán Arab and others, she seized on the person of the Nawáb, and confining him in the Úparkot, proclaimed her grandson Múzafar Khán as Nawáb. Jawán Mard Khán II., the Nawáb of Sami Múnjpúr, observing the anarchy at Júnágadh, and thinking that this would be a good opportunity to unite the two chiefdoms, led a large army against Júnágadh, ostensibly with the design of freeing Máhábat Khán, but really with the intention of carrying him off a prisoner, and after crushing the party of Múzafar Khán and Fatehyab Khán, placing his son Ghází-úd-din Khán in Júnágadh as his deputy, himself returning to Sami. But the Úparkot defied his utmost efforts, and he was forced to withdraw two marches from the town, but halting there, he watched events. At this juncture Jáḍejá Kúmbhoji, the heir to the Gondal State, who was ever anxious to exalt his own influence and weaken the power of Júnágadh, fearing lest the power should pass from the weak hands of Máhábat Khán to the vigorous rule of Jawán Mard Khán, one of the ablest and most ambitious men of the time, prevailed on that noble to retire to Gújarát. He also obtained the liberation of Máhábat Khán, on condition that the estate of Ránpúr should be granted to Múzafar Khán and Fatehyáb Khán in return for their renouncing all claim to share in the chiefdom. It was also stipulated that Bibi Sáhibah Súltán should withdraw from Júnágadh. Jáḍejá Kúmbhoji's influence was naturally at this time paramount, and he managed to have the parganah of Úpletá written over to him in consideration of a sum of Jámshai koris 85,000, which he advanced for the Nawab's immediate necessities, the annual jamá of the parganah payable to the Nawáb being fixed at 5,000 koris.

At this time great anarchy reigned at Júnágadh; though the Nawáb had been liberated, he had no means to maintain a respectable force or to pay responsible ministers, and was forced to maintain his army and such state as he held, by predatory expeditions into the neighbouring districts, paying his soldiers from the booty thus obtained, and gradually established a variable tribute. But this mode of government speedily broke down. The troops fell into arrears, and the Arabs seized on the Úparkot, and vowed to hold it until their demands should be satisfied, while Bibi Sáhibah Súltán seized on Veráwal, from which however she was shortly afterwards expelled by Kázi

Shekh Mián and Malik Shaháb-úd-din, who ruled there with the connivance of Desái Súndarji, in complete independence.

The Nawáb now besieged the Arabs in the Úparkot, and affairs were in this position when the future Diwán Amarji, then a youth of 18, came to Júnágadh from Mángrol, of which place he was a native, in quest of service. The Nawáb promised him service if he could capture the Wágeshwari gate, and Amarji who had brought with him Jamádár Sálmin and a band of Arabs from Porbandar, undertook to do this, and not only captured the Wágeshwari gate, but obtained access to the Úparkot, and after agreeing to pay the refractory Arabs half their demand, compelled them to evacuate. The Nawáb after this signal service employed both Amarji and Jamádár Sálmin in important posts, and Amarji in every appointment gave satisfaction. The Nawáb now sent him against Verával, and he expelled Shekh Mián, &c., imprisoned Súndarji Desái, and enabled the Nawáb to make a triumphal entry.

In about A. D. 1764 Shekh Mián of Mángrol created disturbances in that part of the country. The Diwán Amarji accordingly marched against him, and after much fighting took from him the forts of Sil, Diwásá, Mahiári, and Bagasrá, and then advanced on Mángrol itself, and commenced to cannonade the fort. Shekh Mián finding himself reduced to great straits, agreed to divide his parganah, and give the Nawáb a half share therein, and on these terms peace was concluded.

The Nawáb, however, cherished enmity against his minister, he feared that he was becoming too powerful, and consequently gave ear to those who desired his ruin, and in A. D. 1767 imprisoned both Amarji and his brothers Dúlabhji and Govindji. His next step was to procure the assassination of Jamádár Sálmin, a faithful adherent of the Diwán's. After a confinement of five months he fined Diwán Amarji 40,000 Jámshái koris, and released him and his brethren. The Minister now retired from Júnágadh to Jetpur, and took up his residence there. Shortly after, the Nawáb marched against Shekh Mián of Mángrol, who had been disturbing the country, but was unable to make any impression on him. He therefore invited Amarji to return. Immediately on the Diwán's return to power, Shekh Mián agreed to restore the property he had plundered, and pay a fine, and to be enrolled among the vassals of the Júnágadh State.

After this victory, the Diwánji marched against Sútrápáḍá, and expelled the Zamindár, one Cháud, a Patani Kasbáti by origin, and took possession of the place for the Nawáb. Châud retired for safety to Gorakhmadi, the celebrated shrine of the Kánphata atits.

In about A. D. 1768-69, Ráwal Wakhtsingh of Bhávnagar, who was exceedingly anxious to expel the Báriá Kolis from Táláját, induced the Diwánji to attack that place with him. The attack was made and the Diwánji who exposed himself freely was wounded in the leg. Eventually it was arranged that Táláját should remain in the hands of the Kolis on condition that they should pay a fine. This fine they paid, and the troops retired.

In A. D. 1770 Sherzamán Khán of Bántwá, uncle of Nawáb Máhábat Khán, attacked Júnágadh, but was compelled to retire. In this year Wálá Kúmpo of Jetpur requested Amarji to join him in attacking Dilkhániyáh in the Gir Forest, then a haunt of outlaws, robbers and banditti. Amarji agreed, and proceeding thither, they stormed the place, and scattered the outlaws after much slaughter.

While the army was still at Dilkhániyáh, Pir Khán Sarwáni, and Sáoná Khokhar, Kasbátis of Kútiáná, represented that they had handed Kútiáná over to Háshim Khán considering him to be a son of Nawáb Bahádúr Khán, but that he was sorely oppressing the people, and that they feared lest he might surrender the town to Ráná Súltánji of Porbandar, who was now very powerful. On hearing this, Amarji at once marched to Kútianá, and laid siege to that town, and undermined and blew up one of the principal bastions. Háshim Khán now sued for peace, and received Majhevadi in jágir after surrendering Kútiáná, which town Amarji placed under the charge of his younger brother Govindji, and afterwards went on a tribute-collecting expedition in the neighbouring districts.

Shortly after this he led an expedition against the Miánás of Máliá, whom he chastised and fined, and then marched against the Bábriás, whom he also humbled. On this occasion he met with some opposition from the Kasbátis of Úna, and finally carried off some of the sons of the chief Kasbati Shekh Táhir as prisoners to Júnágadh.

All this time Jáḍejá Kúmbhoji of Gondal, though he had obtained the valuable parganahs of Dhoráji and Úpletá, feared much that Amarji would not let him enjoy them peaceably, but would endeavour to retake them. He was therefore anxious to poison the ear of the Nawáb against him, and succeeded in convincing Máhábat Khán that Amarji was becoming too powerful, and that he aimed at sovereign rule and would eventually depose him. As soon as the Nawáb was prejudiced against Amarji, Kúmbhoji secretly obtained his permission to attack him with the aid of the Maráthá forces which were then in the province. Agreeably to this design, the combined forces of Kúmbhoji and the Maráthás attacked the Diwán's army then camped at Wálásamḍi, but without success, and when the Diwán drew up in order of battle, Kúmbhoji seeing that he had made an error, withdrew from the opposite camp. The Tarikh-i-Sorath says that this conspiracy was principally got up by Bámanioji of Chatrásah, and that the Diwán consequently led his army to Chatrásah to chastise him. But Bámanioji averted his wrath by the payment of a large fine, and by promises to cabal no more against him.

In A. D. 1774 Meráman Khawás, Kárbhári of Jám Jasáji of Nawánagar, invited the Diwán Amarji to co-operate with him in chastising the Okhá Wághers. To this request the Diwán assented, and putting his troops in motion, speedily arrived before the fort of Positra, which place was a perfect storehouse of plunder both from the neighbouring countries by land, and from all vessels passing that way by sea. He now sprung a mine, and immediately after carried the place by assault, and acquired enormous booty. Ere the Diwán had returned from this expedition, and while he was still in Okhá, Nawáb Máhábat Khán died, after a reign of nearly sixteen years and a quarter. His death took place in April 1775.

On hearing this news the Diwán at once returned to Júnágadh, and seated Hámid Khán, then a boy of eight years of age, in his father's seat; and immediately after making proper arrangements for carrying on the government, he went on a múlkgiri expedition, and collected tribute; and in this year he first levied tribute from the country of Jháláwár.

Nawábs Hámid Khán, A. D. 1775-1811.

Now the name of Hámid Khán's mother was Súbhán Kúnwar. This foolish lady was induced to join a party of conspirators, headed by Múkhtár Khán and Edal Khán of Bántwá, and to sanction a rebellion which they raised during Diwán Amarji's absence. Their first step was to corrupt the Kasbátis of Wanthali, and thus they obtained possession of that fort. But ere their rising had become dangerous, Diwán Amarji hastened thither by forced marches. Ere he could reach Wanthali, the rebels invited Abu Rái and Mahipat Ráo, the Súbah of Áhmadábád (who happened at that time to be collecting tribute in the neighbourhood), to join them. On hearing this, the Diwánji marched against the Maráthás. They, finding themselves not sufficiently strong to oppose him, made peace, and handed over to him the tribute they had collected, and entrusted to him the collection of the remainder. The Diwán now concentrated his attack on Wanthali, and speedily reduced the place, only sparing Múkhtár Khán's life on account of his family connection with the Nawáb. Múkhtár Khán accordingly retired in disgrace to Bántwá.

In about A. D. 1776-77 the Súbahdárs of the Peshwá and Gáckwár named Amrat Rao and Thoban respectively, joined forces, and entered the province to collect tribute, but were met by the Diwán Amarji and his army near Jetpur, and a fierce combat ensued, in which the historian of Sorath claims victory for the Diwán, and says that "the Maráthás turned their backs." But it seems probable that the issue of the battle was doubtful; next day through the mediation of Wálá Kánthaḍ of Jetpúr, and

Jádejá Kúmbhoji of Gondal, peace was concluded. An interview was arranged, and presents exchanged, and the Maráthá force returned to Áhmadábád, where shortly after his return Amrat Ráo was assassinated by an Arab.

The Morbi chieftain, whose name was Wághji, now invited Diwán Amarji to join him in an expedition to Wágaḍ. The Diwán assented, and the united armies crossed the Ran, and captured the villages of Pálanswá and Kerianagar. The Ráo now by sending valuable presents and polite messages, averted further war; and the Diwán and Wághji recrossed the Ran.

About the close of A. D. 1777 Jiwáji Shámráj Subahdár on behalf of the Gáekwár entered the province at the head of an army to collect tribute, and camping at Amreli, endeavoured to establish himself there on an independent footing, and with this view attempted to conquer some of the adjacent territory. But the Diwán Amarji perceiving that such a neighbour would prove very troublesome, at once marched against him. Jiwáji was soon so harassed by the constant attacks of the Diwan's forces that he was forced to shut himself up in the fort of Amreli, and stand a siege. But the Diwán pressed the siege so hotly that he was compelled to surrender the place, and to quit the province. The Diwán after this surrender demolished the Amreli fort.

Shekh Mián of Mángrol, who was an ambitious and turbulent man, now commenced exciting disturbances at Mángrol, and the Diwán sent his own brother Dúlabhji against him, and hostilities between Dúlabhji and Shekh Mián continued for several months with equal fortune. In June 1778, the mother of Raghúnáthji, Ranchoḍji, &c., and the wife of Diwán Amarji, died at Júnágadh. Shekh Mián took advantage of this occasion to come to terms, and accordingly paid the Diwánji a visit of condolence at Júnágadh, and on promising to offend no more, his past excesses were overlooked.

At the close of A. D. 1778, Fatehsingh Ráo Gáekwár, anxious to retrieve the disaster which had befallen his lieutenant Jiwáji Shámráj, invaded the peninsula at the head of a large and well appointed army, and advanced as far as Jetpúr. Here, however, some of the neighbouring chieftains intervoned, and the Gáekwár, abandoning his design of avenging himself, sent to the Diwánji handsome dresses of honour, and further forgave him the jamábandi in arrear. He again invaded the province in A. D. 1779 with a similar intent, but finding himself unable to cope with Diwán Amarji, was compelled to retire without accomplishing his purpose.

About this time Ráná Súltánji of Porbandar, at the instigation of his minister, a Loháná named Premji, commenced disturbances in Bardá, and the Diwánji, with a view to checking this in the bud, marched at once against him, but the Ráná conscious of his own inferiority, averted his wrath by timely submission, and by presenting him with certain costly articles which had fallen into his hands from a vessel wrecked on his coast, together with a tribute in excess of the usual amount.

While the Diwán's forces were still in this direction, Jáḍejá Kúmbhoji of Gondal represented that certain Sindhis, headed by one Malik Muhammad and others, resided in the forts of Devrá and Khágasri, and thence ravaged his parganahs, which he said in fact were those of Júnágadh, and besought the Diwán to expel them. Diwán Amarji, reinforced from Kútianá by the forces of his younger brother Govindji, marched against the forts in question, and took them, expelling the Sindhis. In this year A. D. 1780 there was some scarcity in Káthiáwár, but it was fortunatoly of but short duration.

In 1782 A. D. the Diwán led an army against Shekh Táhir, the Kasbáti of Úná and Delwáḍá, and conquered these places, granting two villages in inám to Shekh Táhir. After the conquest, he left a Bánswárá Nágar named Parbháshankar as foujdár there, and the Tárikh-i-Sorath says of him that he, after much trouble, "rooted out the stock of the accursed Bábriás and reduced them to submission and obedience," so that it would seem that though Shekh Táhir ruled at the capital of this parganah, many of the villages were held by Bábriás. The prowess of Parbháshankar was so great that the above quoted history relates that both the Habshi of Muzafarábád (Jáfarábád) and the Faringhi of Div feared Parbháshankar greatly, and were obliged to be constantly on the alert lest he should attack them.

Hitherto the administration of Diwán Amarji had been a brilliant series of successes. Through him Júnágadh had become the premier state in the province, and he had both revived the old foujdárs' right of tribute, and withheld payment of tribute to the Gáekwár, whose officers he had on more than one occasion signally humbled. He had reduced the neighbouring chieftains to submission, had conquered many of the separate holdings held by kasbátis or thánahdárs of the Moghal Empire, who on the dissolution of the imperial power had become independent, and added their estates to the Júnágadh dominions, and his alliance was courted by all the neighbouring chieftains. It is possible that he may have even dreamed of himself becoming the monarch of Sorath, though at present he considered it wise to continue wielding the real power during Hámid Khán's minority, and contended himself with exercising authority in his name. However this may be, he had no doubt raised the Babi kingdom of Júnágadh to a higher pre-eminence than it had previously reached, but in doing so he had made several bitter foes. The most dangerous of these was Jádejá Kúmbhoji of Gondal, a daring, able and ambitious man, who saw that while Amarji lived, his hold on the parganahs of Dhoráji and Upletá could never be reckoned secure. He never relaxed intriguing against the minister, and formed combination after combination to crush him, all of which however proved unsuccessful, until by insidious suggestions to Nawáb Hámid Khán he prompted him to procure his assassination. Kúmbhoji now found an excellent opportunity to form a league against Amarji, and persuaded Merámau Khawás, the powerful minister of Nawánagar, to unite with him and Ráná Sáltánji of Porbandar (whom the Diwán had recently humbled) to crush the power of Amarji.

With this intent the three confederates and other petty chieftains in A.D. 1782 poured their forces into the Kútiáná district, and commenced to harry the villages and carry off the crops. The Diwánji, however, was not a whit dismayed, and marched to Jetpúr against them. At this time it so happened that

Merámau Khawás' army, and that of the Zamindárs, was encamped on the southern bank of the river Bhádar. Foreseeing that it would be difficult to cross the Bhádar with an active enemy in his neighboured, Merámau Khawás sent wakils to amuse the Diwán, while secretly he re-crossed the Bhádar and retired to Pánchpiplá, where he entrenched himself. The Diwánji, however, pursued him thither, and a battle was fought in which the Diwán obtained some advantage. The force of Mánáji Gáekwár (brother of Fatehsing Ráo) however was in the neighbourhood, and Merámau Khawás besought its aid, and Mánáji assenting, the Diwán deemed it prudent to retire. In the battle of Pánchpiplá, Shekh Mián of Mángrol fought on the side of the Diwán, and in the language of the local history "flashed like lightning on the threshing floor of the enemy."

In spite however of the aid of the Gáekwár army, the Zamindárs and Merámau dared not pursue him, but contended themselves with storming the fort of Devrá, a task which they easily accomplished, and after destroying the fortifications and plundering the place, the Gáekwár army returned to Baroda. This was the signal for the dissolution of the league, Merámau Khawás returned to Nawánagar, and Ráná Súltánji and Kúmbhoji to their respective capitals.

The Diwán, however, gave them but little time to repose, he first attacked Ráná Súltánji and laid waste his territory. Merámau Khawás, fearing his turn might be the next, propitiated the minister with apologies and payments, and actually sent a force to work under his orders against his former allies. Heavy tribute, and a fine was exacted from the Ráná, who was also compelled to repair the fort of Devrá at his own cost.

Then the Diwán sent a force to collect the tribute of Jháláwár and Gohilwár, and proposed on his return to crush Jádejá Kúmbhoji.

It, however, fell out that Nawáb Hámid Khán, who was desirous of returning to the pleasures of the capital, and who resented the supremacy of Amarji, in A.D. 1784, feigning sickness, left the army and returned to Júnágadh. Kúmbhoji perceiving his opportunity, induced the Nawáb to be his guest at Gondal for a night on his way, and on the Nawáb consenting, he used so well all the arts of which he was master to poison the ears of the young chief against his minister, that he induced him to plot the assassination of the Diwán. In this matter Kúmbhoji not only bribed lavishly all the Nawáb's confidants, but he promised to pay the Nawáb himself a sum of three lákhs of Jámnagar koris when the death of the Diwán should be announced to him. A conspiracy was soon set on foot, and when the Diwánji returned to Júnágadh in March 1784 to celebrate the Holi-festival, it was resolved to put the plan in execution. Accordingly the widow of the late Nawáb Máhábat Khán invited him to her palace on pretence of showing him the jewels and trousseau of the daughter of the Nawáb of Rádhanpur, and while there he was put to death on the 6th March 1784, and his relations in Júnágadh, viz., his brother Dúlabhji, his son Ranchoḍji and others, were imprisoned.

But the Arab Jamádárs and others who owed much to the late Diwán, did all in their power to mitigate the severity of their imprisonment. The army of the Gáekwár, under the command of Morár Ráo Gáekwár, was at this time in Gohilwár, and with it was Rúpoji Sindhia, a cousin of Máhádáji Sindhiá, with whom the late Diwán had been personally acquainted. They on the entreaties of the relations of the murdered man and others, marched to Dhandhúsar about eight miles from Júnágadh, and called upon the Nawáb to release the relations of Amarji whom he had placed in confinement. The Arab Jamadárs, also despairing of being paid their arrears, confined the Nawáb to his palace until their claims should be satisfied. Under this pressure the Nawáb was forced to yield, and after a month's confinement he released the relations of his late minister.

As soon as the vigorous hand of Amarji was cold in death, the neighbouring zamindárs seized on the opportunity to encroach, and Ráwal Wakhtsingh of Bhávnagar expelled the Júnágadh thánah recently placed in Máhúwá and took possession of that place, and shortly afterwards obtained possession of Loliáná, Pátnó, and Salḍi.

The Gáekwár's army remained at Dhandhúsar until the Nawáb should promise satisfaction to the family of the murdered minister, and finally in A.D. 1784 an arrangement was drawn up, which it is unnecessary to quote here at length, whereby certain villages were granted to them, and certain parganahs mortgaged to them until the debt of 60 lákhs of Jámshái koris due to the Diván Amarji should be repaid to them. This agreement was drawn up through the intervention of the Gáekwár, and the securities were certain Syads, and Arab and Sindhi Jamádárs. In addition to this Raghúnáthji, son of the deceased minister, was appointed minister. The Gáekwár forces now retired, but the Arabs kept the Nawáb confined to his tents, which were pitched near the Wanthali gate of the town, until security should be given them for the payment of their arrears of salary. The Nawáb, however, evaded their vigilance in disguise, and returning to the city, commenced to cannonade his refractory troops, and a compromise was arranged whereby half their demands were paid and the rest were cancelled by them.

The deceased Diwán's brother Dúlabhji and others of the family, seeing that intrigues were afoot to oust Raghúnáthji, retired with their families to Jetpúr, whence Dúlabhji left for Úná. Shortly after this the Nawáb induced the garrison of Veráwal (which was in the hands of the Diwán Raghúnáthji) to side with him, and they delivered over the fort and expelled Ragúnáthji, who then joined his uncle at Jetpúr. The Nawáb's advisers now counselled him to deprive the Diwán's family of the parganahs, &c., in their possession, and accordingly in 1785 the thánahdár of the Diwán was driven away from Sútrápáḍá, but Mehtá Parbháshankar proceeded thither, and reinstated the Diwán's rule, and Ranchoḍji (the author of the Tárikh-i-Sorath) was installed then in command, but he was expelled shortly after Govindji, another brother of the late Diwán Amarji, was at this time forced to quit Júnágadh, and he joined the rest of his family at Jetpúr. The Nawáb now used every effort to corrupt Parbháshankar, and he, seeing the fortunes of the house of Amarji fallen so low, finally accepted the Nawáb's overtures and drove Dúlabhji from Úná. Dúlabhji first went to Dhoráji and then joined the rest of his family at Jetpúr. Here Jáḍejá Kúmbhoji, whose constant aim was to foment dissensions in Júnágadh and weaken the power of the Nawáb, so that the parganahs of Dhoráji and Úpletá might remain in his hands, now made polite overtures to the late Diwán's family, and offered them every assistance.

Meanwhile in A.D. 1786, the jamádárs of the mercenaries, (Arabs, Sindhis, and others,) finding the control of Diwán Amarji removed, endeavoured to become independent. A band of Sindhis seized upon Wanthali, while Jamádárs Karamsháh, Gúlsháh, &c., held the Rang-Mahál palace at Júnágadh. The Nawáb, by a secret understanding with some of the Arabs, procured the assassination of Jamádár Gúlsháh, and effected the expulsion of Jamádár Karamsháh, &c., from Júnágadh. They at once repaired to Wanthali, where the Sindhi rebels received them with open arms. From this strong position the Nawáb endeavoured in vain to dislodge them, though at one time he made overtures to Loháná Premji, Kárbhári of the Ráná of Porbandar, to assist him. But the negotiation fell through, and finally, the Nawáb was obliged to solicit Diwáns Dúlabhji and Raghúnáthji to return to his service and take office, and in this year the Nawáb married the daughter of Nawáb Ghází-ud-din Khán of Sami-Múnjpúr at Morbi, with much pomp.

No sooner were the Diwáns Dúlabhji and Raghúnáthji restored to power, than they proceeded to subdue the refractory throughout the Nawáb's dominions. At this time it so fell out that Sangji Ráizádáh, the Zamindár of Chorwár, was slain in battle at Máliá, and the Ráná of Porbandar, on pretence of being related to him, and by agreeing to pay the demands of the merceneries, obtained possession of the place, and in A.D. 1788 he surprised and captured the fort of Verávwal. The Nawáb with his ministers now proceeded in person to quell these disturbances, and after a gallant resistance, captured the fort of Chorwár. On this occasion Jáḍejá Kúmbhoji of Gondal served with the Nawáb's forces and obtained permission that Mokáji Ráizádáh, the zamindár of Chorwár and his family, should be allowed to retire to Dhoráji without molestation. The Nawáb next proceeded to Veráwál, which place also he soon made himself master of, and then proceeded to levy tribute. This done, and funds being collected, he marched to chastise the Ráná of Porbandar, and compelled him to pay a nazaránah and fine, and thus purchase his forbearance. The Kasbátis of Sútrápáḍá, who had previously expelled the Diwán Ranchoḍji from thence at the Nawáb's instigation, had now thrown off his yoke, and held the whole parganah in their hands. They were now driven forth, and the Diwán Ranchodji reinstated in the command there. Misunderstandings now sprung up between the Nawáb and Diwán Ranchodji, and the latter for a period of six months retired from office, but after that time he at the urgent solicitation of the Nawáb returned to power. While, however, the misunderstanding lasted, *i.e.* in about 1787 A.D. Jáḍejá Kúmbhoji of Gondal contrived to obtain a writing from the Nawáb permanently granting him in perpetuity* Gondal and Jetalsar, Meli and Majethi, Láth and Bhimorá, as well as the parganah of Sarsái and Chámpardá in consideration of the sum of three lákhs of Jámshái koris which he had lent the Nawáb in A.D. 1774 and which the Nawáb was unable to repay him.

In the meantime Dághoji Ráizádáh, Zamindar of Kesoj, entertaining a large body of mercenaries, commenced to plunder the adjacent villages and finally ventured to attack and plunder the town of Bántwá. On this Edal Khán and Múkhtiár Khán Bábi besought aid from Diwán Raghúnáthji, who despatched his uncle Dúlabhji and his brother Ranchodji to their aid, and they joining the Bábis of Bántwá, fought several times with Dághoji and finally compelled him to sue for peace and restore the plunder of Bántwá, and also pay a fine. Finally, Dághoji being unable to pay the arrears of his mercenaries, was compelled to sell the fort and town of Kesoj to the Nawáb for a lákh of Jámshái koris in A.D. 1788.

---

* Gondal was an original possession of Kúmbhoji's, but what he now probably obtained from the Nawáb was a formal admission of his rights.

At this time the pay of the Arab soldiery was much in arrears, and as the Nawáb would not defray their demands, the Arabs confined him strictly to the Rang Mahál palace. The Nawáb, however, eluded their vigilance, and collected a force outside the city and ignominiously expelled the rebellious Arabs. The new conquest of Chorwár, too, was held by other Arab mercenaries until their salary in arrears should be paid, but as no attempts were made to satisfy them, they issued thence and commenced to ravage the country. Sámalji, maternal uncle of the local historian Ranchodji, was sent with a force to Chorwár to check them, and at this time, viz., early in A.D. 1790, Diwán Govindji died. In this year hail fell, and did much damage to the crops. Next year, viz. A.D. 1791, the peninsula was visited by famine, which was aggravated by a severe outburst of small-pox which caused terrible loss of life. All these misfortunes were heightened at Chorwár by the ravages of the Arabs, but they were finally dislodged and the fort recovered, and Diwán Ranchodji was placed in command there. In this year Jamádár Hámid Sindhi came in command of the Gáekwár's forces to levy tribute, and laid waste the country as far as Verával, but owing to the famine and sickness, &c., was able to levy but little. Finally, when on his return in A.D. 1792 he passed within eight miles of Júnágadh, the Júnágadh forces attacked him. In the conflict which ensued Jamádár Hámid was slain and his forces compelled to beat a hasty retreat.

Although the Júnágadh State had been greatly benefited by the conquests and good management of the late Diwán Amarji, and his brothers' and sons' good administration after him, nevertheless Nawáb Hámid Khán was ever distrustful of them, and ready to listen to the suggestions of their enemies. Amongst these were Jaḍejá Kúmbhoji of Gondal, who preferred to see them in opposition to, rather than in concert with, the Nawáb; and numerous intriguing persons of the official class at the capital who desired to enjoy the sweets of office. Accordingly in A.D. 1793 the Nawáb, at the advice of Kalián Seth and others of Júnágadh, imprisoned the Diwan Raghúnáthji, his brother Morarji, Parbháshankar, Dyálji, and other Nágars, and plundered their houses, and thus obtained all their wealth. In the meantime their brother Ranchodji openly went into rebellion, and captured both Kodinár and Pátan. After an imprisonment of six months the Nawáb put to death Parbháshankar and Dyálji, who were the principal agents of the Diwán's family, but released both Raghúnathji and Morárji without any fine. Ranchodji now entered the service of the Jám and obtained the parganahs of Pardhari and Átkot in jagir. Dúlabhji retired to Bhávnagar, where he received four villages in jagir. The son of Govindji, who was named Mangalji, was of tender age, and most of his property was confiscated by way of fine, but afterwards he for a short time served Ráná Súltánji of Porbandar, and afterwards Jám Jasáji with a regiment of cavalry. The Nawáb now, at the instigation of Kalián Seth, who was a Wániá by caste, exacted a fine of 10 lákhs of Jámshai koris from the Nágar and Somparah Bráhmans of Júnágadh, and Kalián Seth and Mádhavrái Khúshálrái, a Nágar of Gújarát, were appointed joint ministers. In A.D. 1794 Ráwal Wakhtsingh of Bhávnagar chastised the Káthis of Chital, although they were dependents of Júnágadh, and expelled the Júnágadh thánáh from that town. After a short time dissensions arose between Kalián Seth and Mádhavrái, and the latter fleeing from Júnágadh, seized on the town of Wanthali. The Nawáb now asked the Diwán Raghúnáthji for aid, and he sent his brother Ranchodji with a force against Mádhavrái, who now surrendered the fort and went to Gondal, Ranchodji returning to Nawánagar.

In June 1795, Prince Bahádúr Khán was born, his mother being Rájkúnwarbái. In 1796 Jamádár Fateh Muhammad, the Bhúj minister, invaded Hálár with a large army. Meráman Khawás entreated the assistance of the Nawáb, who joined him with a large army at the village of Dhensará under Morbi. Kalián Seth, who was now Diwán of Júnágadh, accompanied the army, but peace was concluded through the efforts of the Ráj Sáhib of Halwad, Diwán Raghúnáthji on behalf of Nawánagar, and Kalián Seth on the part of Júnágadh, and the Kachh army retired without doing further damage.

The Nawáb Sáhib now resolved to chastise Ráwal Wakhtsingh of Bhávnagar, who had seized on Rájúlá and Kúndlá, and accordingly he proceeded thither with a large army which was soon swelled by the malcontents against Bhávnagar. At first he was successful, capturing Kúndlá from the Bhávnagar Thánahdár Morárji, son of Diwán Dúlabhji, and after a gallant resistance he also conquered the fort of Rájúlá, taking Káyábhái Gohil prisoner. Thence he advanced into Bhávnagar territory, and laid waste the country as far as Waral, where Wakhatsinghji met him, and a doubtful battle was fought, but the Nawáb thought it advisable to retire towards Chital and Láthi. This retreat was made, it is said, at the advice of Kalián Seth, and greatly discouraged the Júnágadh troops and their Káthi allies, while it elated the Bhávnagar army, which advanced to the southern frontier of Dhasá within easy distance of the Nawáb's camp at Jharkhiá. Here battle was joined, and though both sides fought with great constancy for a whole day without either army gaining the advantage, Kalián Seth advised the Nawáb to conclude peace with Ráwal Wakhatsingh. Peace was now concluded on the bases of a payment by Ráwal Wakhatsingh of one lákh and fifteen thousand rupees and the cession of the parganahs of Kúndlá and Rájúlá by the Nawáb. This happened in A. D. 1796. Kalián Seth was much blamed for his cowardly counsel by the Júnágadh nobles, and was shortly after much harassed by the soldiery for the payment of their arrears of salary.

About this time Máliá was wrested from the Háti grásiá of that place and added to the crown possessions of Júnágadh. Now Shivrám Gárdi had entered the province in A. D. 1795 and levied treble the amount of tribute usually collected, as he was unopposed, as was usual by the Júnágadh forces. Ámin Sáhib, son of Jamádár Hámid, who had been killed near Júnágadh in A. D. 1792 during Diván Raghúnáthji's tenure of power, observing the dissensions of the chiefs and the weakness of Júnágadh, obtained permission from the Gáekwár to lead an army into the peninsula and to take revenge for his father. Accordingly in A. D. 1798 he led a force against Majhevaḍi, about seven miles from Júnágadh, and broke down the battlements of the fort with his cannon, and only returned after he had levied a triple tribute as had been done by Shivrám Gárdi.

This inroad straitened the resources at Kalián Seth's disposal for paying the troops more than ever, and with a view to employing them and at the same time of raising funds, he led them against Dhándhalpúr in the Panchál, which fort was defended by Godad Khavaḍ. But he miscalculated his strength, the Káthis harassed his camp with constant sallies, and their kinsmen in the neighbouring villages cut off all supplies until the Júnágadh forces were forced to retire. The troops now became very clamorous against Kalián Seth, who was forced to take them to Kûtiáná, and thence ravage the surrounding districts of Porbandar, Drápha, and Hálár, and thus defray their demands. Kalián Seth now appears to have thought of rebellion, and he was joined at Kûtiáná by Múkhtiár Khán Bábi of Bántwá, and their ravages extended far and wide, until the Nawáb became apprefour villages and a half share of the town of Máliá was retained by him, the rest of the tálûkah being annexed by Júnágadh. Dhanej is said to have been granted to Sájan Dhakel, an Avartia Hátti by one of the Chûdásama Rás of Júnágadh, for assistance given to him on the occasion of the siege and capture of Bet and Dwárká. Some of this man's descendants still hold land in Dhanej. The Háttis are called by the bards Mewádás, as though they came from Mewád (Mewar). There are about 500 or 600 houses of Háttis in the Júnágadh territory, some of which are in the Mángrol villages.

Diwán Raghúnáthji now, entrusting the charge of Kútiáná to his brother Ranchoḍji, set out in company with Kúnwar Dewoji of Gondal on a tribute levying expedition, and proceeding to Jháláwár, collected tribute as far as Limbḍi. During his absence, Ranchoḍji compelled the garrisons of Úná and Chorwár (which places were held by the adherents of Kalián Seth) to evacuate those forts and hand them over to the custody of the Nawáb. He then marched to join the Diwán Raghúnáthji at Limbḍi.

In A. D. 1803 Ranchoḍji again sallied forth with an army to

collect tribute, and levied double the usual amount in Jháláwár, where however he was opposed, though ineffectually, by Shivrám Gárdi on the part of the Gáekwár.

At this time Múkand Ráo Gáekwár, who commanded the forces of the Gáekwár at Amreli, rebelled against his sovereign, and to raise funds imprisoned the Wasáwaḍ desayas. Ranchoḍji, however, at the request of the desayas, released them and expelled Múkand Ráo from Amreli.

In A. D. 1804 Bábáji Ápáji, the Diwán of the Gáekwár government, entered the peninsula with a large army, and commenced to levy three times what Shivrám Gárdi had levied: nevertheless, though Ranchoḍji was not strong enough to engage him in a pitched battle, he compelled him to raise the siege of Wanthali, and harassed him so much that he restored the written bonds and promises to pay tribute which he had extorted from the villages for exorbitant amounts, and took only tribute according to the custom of the country. The Tárikh-i-Sorath however admits that from the time of Bábáji, the tribute of Káthiáwár was trebled.

Diwán Raghúnáthji apparently now found it necessary to remain in Júnágaḍh to counteract the intrigues of those evilly disposed to him, and consequently usually entrusted the comless, though Ranchoḍji was not strong enough to engage him in a pitched battle, he compelled him to raise the siege of Wanthali, and harassed him so much that he restored the of Kûtiáná to Diwán Raghûnáthji part of the Gáekwár.

In A.D. 1806, after the departure f the Diwán Raghûnáthji for Kûtiáná, the other officials of the Nawáb dared not for fear of Bábáji Ápáji take an army to levy tribute, and in the cold weather of 1807 Colonel Walker accompanied Bábáji Ápáji's force and concluded the permanent settlement of the tribute of the Káthiáwár Chieftains. It seems that Vithal Ráo, the Gáekwár's Diwán, was very hostile to the Diwán Raghúnáthji, but Colonel Walker befriended him and the family of Diwán Amarji. Colonel Walker remained in the province till 1809, and in 1811 Nawáb Sáhib Hámid Ḳhán died.

Hámid Khán was succeeded by his son Bahádúr Khán, who was then 18 years of age. He was brought up at Pátan, and was brought to Júnágadh by Káhándás and Jamádár Omar Mûkhásam and Ázam Beg Chelá and seated on his father's throne. After this Jamádár Omar Mûkhásam became a man of great influence in the Nawáb's darbar.

Nawáb Sáhib Bahádúr Khan, A.D. 1811-1840.

Shortly after the accession of Nawáb Sáhib Bahádûr Khán, Omar Múkhásam and other chief men of Júnágadh came to Kûtiáná and besought the Diwán Sáhib Raghúnáthji to take up the post of Diwán, and after some hesitation he accepted the appointment. In A.D. 1812 the English and Gáekwár armies marched against Nawánagar and humbled the Jám, and immediately after this they advanced on Júnágadh, and encamping at Lálwaḍ, about eight miles from Júnágadh, demanded a nazaránáh by way of succession duty from Nawáb Bahádûr Khán. Diwán Raghûnáthji, on his part, strengthened the fort and prepared for a siege. When, however, the Diwán met Captain Carnac and Gangádhar Shástri, he saw at once the importance of being on good terms with the British and Gáekwár Governments, and accompanied Captain Carnac and Gangádhar Shástri to Amreli (where he was invited by the latter to attend his wedding with Vithal Ráo Dewáji's daughter) with a view of arranging relations between Júnágadh and the Governments in question. The enemies of the Diwán Raghûnáthji took advantage of this absence of his at Amreli, to prejudice the Nawáb Sáhib against him, and persuaded him that Raghûnáthji was about to sacrifice his interests to the British and Gáekwár Governments, and caused him to write secretly to the Gáekwári authorities saying that they should now leave off negotiations, as the Diwán was opposed to any terms being arranged, but that afterwards he (the Nawáb) would agree to whatever they wished. On being shown this, Diwán Raghúnáthji saw that further negotiation was now impossible, and accordingly he left Amreli and returned to Júnágadh. Having arrived here, he and his brother Ranchoḍji had an interview with the Nawáb's mother Rájkunwarbái, who in reality conducted all important State matters, and asked her whether they should comply or not with the Gáekwár's demand. She replied, at the advice of her counsellers, in a loud voice and said, "We "will not give even a span's breadth of land, but if it be abso-"lutely necessary to pay a moderate nazaránáh in money, it "will not matter."

On hearing this the Diwán Raghûnáthji, who had apparently pledged himself to cede a few villages, threw up office and retired from the Ministry. Immediately on his withdrawal from power, Vithal Ráo Dewánji commenced to corrupt Jamádár Omar Mokhásam and the Bái's private Kárbháris with bribes, and thus obtained from Nawáb Bahádur Khán a deed writing over to the Gáekwár the parganahs of Amreli and Koḍinár. Vithal Ráo at once rebuilt the Amreli fort, and soon extended his power over several of the neighbouring small tálûkahs.

In A.D. 1813 a comet appeared in the heavens, and in the same year the rains were so scanty that there was a famine in the land, which was followed in 1814 by a severe attack of pestilence from which many persons died.

A year or two after this, Captain Ballantyne visited Káthiáwár, and about this time (says the author of the Tárikh-i-Sorath) the Nawáb's advisers persuaded him to resume the Maháls granted to the Diwán's family in form, and to grant them in lieu thereof the four villages of Khágasri, Iswariá, Meswáua, and Wáḍásárá in jágir on the security of the English and Gáekwár Governments. At this time there were apparently two great parties in Káthiáwár—one represented by Vithal Ráo Dewáji, who may have aimed at asserting his independence although he acted in the Gáekwár's name. He was strongly opposed to the Diwán Raghûnáthji, and directed all his efforts towards the disintegration of the Júnágadh State and his own aggrandizement. The other party was that of Súndarji Shavji, the native agent of the British Government, who had, it is said, much influence over Captain Ballantyne. This person was unfavourably disposed to Vithal Ráo, and favourably inclined to the family of the Diwán.

In A.D. 1815-16 Jamádár Omar Múkhásam, who was a great ally of Vithal Ráo's, attempted violence to the Nawáb, but his guards interposing, the Jamádár was driven from the palace; he now occupied a threatening position in his mansion in the town. The Nawáb becoming seriously alarmed at his attitude, sought counsel and aid from the Diwán Raghûnáthji, who despatched his brother Ranchodji in A.D. 1816 to obtain the assistance of the British. Captain Ballantyne, persuaded both by Sûndarji and by the eloquent appeal of Ranchodji, marched to Júnágadh and expelled Jamádár Omar Múkhásam and other hostile leaders from that city. On this occasion, through Captain Ballantyne's recommendation, the Nawáb Bahádúr Khán reappointed Raghûnáthji as Diwán, and Jamádár Umar received the villages of Timbri and Pipliá and one-and-a-half lákhs of Jámshái koris. Hasan Ábubakar received 40,000 Jámshái koris, and Salim bin Hamid the village of Sángáwárá, and on receiving these they wrote acquittances to the Nawáb of their several claims. The Nawáb, by way of gratitude to the British Government for their assistance in expelling Omar Mûkhásam, gave a writing to the Honourable East India Company, dated A.D. 1817, in which he consents to waive for ever his right to zortalabi from both Dhandhúká, Ránpur, Goghá, and Dholerá. In 1821 an agreement was made by the Nawáb in which he consented that the English should collect his zortalabi throughout the province, and retain one-fourth of the amount collected on account of the expense of recovering the same.

Shortly after this, however, Sûndarji Shavji, relying on Captain Ballantyne's favour, aspired to be Diwán himself, and with this design he set the Nawáb against Diwán Raghúnáthji, and persuaded him that were he Diwán he would recover Dhoráji and Úpletá, and acquire Mángrol, as well as obtain acquittances from the State officials, whose demands amounted to fifty lakhs of Jámshái koris, and also recover the estate of Bálásinor (Wádásinor). In all his intrigues for power Sûndarji had the support of the British Government, and finally was appointed Diwán in A.D. 1818. Subsequently to this, viz. in A.D. 1819, there was a severe earthquake in Káthiáwár, which caused much alarm throughout the province, and in this same year the Diwán Raghúnáthji died.

In 1820 the Gáekwár agreed to make no demands on the Chiefs save through the British Government, and thus the paramount power which had been exercised by the Gáekwár's Súbah at Amreli during the past few years was transferred to the British Government.

Consequent on this Captain Barnewall was appointed Political Agent in Káthiáwár, and proceeded to that province, where, however, the government was actually conducted by the Gáekwár's Súbahdár up to A.D. 1822.

In 1820 the Nawáb Sáhib Bahádúr Khán married a daughter of the Ráo of Kachh (named Kesarbái), and Captain Barnewall and his native agent Chotamlál Bápábhái, a Nágar Bráhman of Áhmadábád, attended the wedding. In 1821 Súndarji Sangvi of Júnágadh and Dhoraji acquired much influence at Júnágadh.

In about A.D. 1822 an English officer of the name of Grant was captured by Wálá Báwá Ráning, a Káthi, and carried off into the hills, but was restored through means of the Nawáb, who granted the Káthi a share in the Visáwadar parganah. Shortly afterwards the said Báwá Ráning was killed in an affray, and his share of Visáwadar reverted to the Darbár. About this time Súndarji Shavji died, and the Nawáb, who was dissatisfied with him on account of his failure to recover Bálásinor and other matters, expelled his son from Júnágadh. During this year one Ahmad Khán, spiritual preceptor of the Nawáb, was assassinated, and two villages were granted in jágir to his son Yusuf Khán.

The soldiery of Júnágadh having now no employment, commenced to make plundering expeditions into the neighbouring villages and towns, and especially annoyed Dhoráji. To such a pitch were these outrages carried, that in about A.D. 1824 Captain Barnewall found it necessary to despatch Mr. Blane with a military force to put a stop to these incursions and enforce the giving of compensation by the Nawáb. Finally the Nawáb made restitution, and further paid a fine of 6,85,000 Jámshái koris. This occurred during the Diwáni of Govindji Jhálá. The leader of these forays was one Jemal Khánt; he was eventually captured and fined 20,000 koris.

In A.D. 1825 there was a famine in Káthiáwár and many cattle died. Captain Barnewall's wife died in 1826, and shortly afterwards he proceeded on leave to the Cape, whence he went to England, and in A.D. 1828 was succeeded as Political Agent by Mr. Blane. In 1834 Sadáshiva Ráo was appointed Diwán of Júnágadh, and in this year the Nawáb sent a strong force against the Baloch of Khaḍiá, who had been plundering the country, and reduced him to submission. In A.D. 1835 Amratlál Amarchand, elder brother of the notorious Ánantji Amarchand, became Diwán, and was succeeded in this office in 1836 by Nathúrám Amarji Búch. In A.D. 1838 the Nawáb Sáhib, at the advice of the English, abolished the rite of sati in his dominions. In 1840 Nawáb Sáhib Bahádúr Khán died, and was succeeded by his eldest son Hámid Khán.

Nawáb Hámid Khán 2nd, A.D. 1840-1851.

Nawáb Hámid Khán 2nd succeeded his father in 1840, at which time Mr. Blane was Political Agent in the province on behalf of the British Government. Hámid Khán was 12 years of age at the time of his accession, and his Chief Minister was Ánantji Amarchand. Hámid Khán was a very promising youth, and was very fond of hunting and the chase, while in all matters of state he displayed great candour and moderation. He discovered a plot in which a false announcement was made that one of his wives had borne a son and punished the authors of it, after unmasking their intrigue. In his time the Júnágadh State papers were arranged in proper order, and regular departments of State were opened, and whereas formerly it had been customary to hear complaints verbally, and give verbal orders, in his time it was first ordained, that written petitions should be given in by applicants for redress, and written orders recorded on such petitions. In 1847 Vidhá Mánik, a Wágher of Okhá, and Rabári Rúdo, who were outlaws, shot Captain Loch as he was travelling to Porbandar. In 1849 Rabári Rúdo was captured, and shortly afterwards Vidhá Mánik surrendered. In 1850 very heavy rain fell in the Júnágadh districts, and many villages were washed away by the rivers. This promising young Chief died of a galloping consumption in A.D. 1851, in the twenty-third year of his age. He was succeeded by his brother Máhábat Khán, the late Nawáb.

Nawáb Sir Máhábat Khán, K.C.S.I., A.D. 1851.

Muhammad Máhábat Khán, at the time of his brother's death, was residing at Rádhanpúr, and was about fourteen years of age. He at once returned to Júnágadh and mounted the gadi. By the advice of the Political Agent, Colonel Lang, the affairs of the State were conducted by a Council presided over by Ánantji Amarchand, until the Nawáb should attain the age of twenty-one years. As soon as he arrived at that age he appointed Ánantji Amarchand and Miá Hámad as his ministers, and conducted affairs himself. He married three wives, viz. (1) Kamál Bakhtá, a daughter of the late Nawáb of Rádhanpúr Zoráwar Khánji, and sister of the present Nawáb; (2) Sardár Bakhtá, daughter of Bábi Sámat Khán of Ránpúr; (3) Láḍḍi Bibi, daughter of Shekh Hásambhái, a resident of Júnágadh. The Nawáb Sáhib in 1856 declared that his wife Kamál Bakhtá's son Áhmad Khán was no son of his, and he was accordingly pronounced spurious by Government. Kamál Bakhtá now retired to Rádhanpúr and died there. Sardár Bakhtá bore no children and died. Láḍḍi Bibi has had one son, Bahádúr Khánji, born in A.D. 1856, who has been recognized by Government as the heir to the estate, but Láḍḍi Bibi herself died in 1864. The Nawáb has also two sons and a daughter by concubines, viz. (1) Rasúl Khán, by a concubine named Núr Bibi, he was born in A.D. 1858 and is therefore now about 20 years of age; (2) Edal Khán, by a concubine name Chhotibú, he was born in A.D. 1867, he is therefore now about 17 years of age and is at present prosecuting his studies in the Rajkúmár College at Rájkot; (3) a daughter named Táj Bakhtá, whose mother's name is Nánibú. She was born in A.D. 1859, and was married to Bábi Sherbúland Khán of Bántwá in A. D. 1873.

When the Nawáb Sáhib succeeded to the gádi he was but 14 years of age, hence great power remained in the hands of his mother Nájú Bibi and her favourite, a woman named Cháitibú. As they were opposed to the Karbhar of Anantji and Miáh Hámad, they made strong representations against this measure to the Political Agent in the name of the Nawáb, and the Political Agent decided that there should again be a Council of Regency. Captain Shortt accordingly was sent to Júnágadh in 1859 with instructions to direct the Sibandi, &c., not to obey any orders of the Nawáb but only those of the Council of Regency. As however they did not comply, Captain Shortt reported to Government through Major Black, and Government sent Mr. Kinloch Forbes as Political Agent in 1860, and through him Dúngarshi Devshi was appointed minister, and Ánantji and Miáh Hámad were persuaded to resign. At this time two Lohánás, Keshavji and Virji, confidential servants of Cháitibú and Nájú Bibi, had acquired great power in the State, and hence Dúngarshi Shet's ministry was carried on smoothly for only four months, and eventually after holding power for fourteen months he was obliged to resign in A.D. 1861, and Jhálá Gokulaji Sampattirám was appointed minister. Afterwards Dúngarshi Shet was implicated in sheltering the Wághers, and was also accused of instigating the murderer of one Dosá Párakh. The actual murderer was tried and hung, and Dúngarshi Shet was prohibited from any intercourse with the agency. In the investigation which took place, some papers were found implicating Keshavji, Miáh Hámad, and others, and they were placed in confinement at Rájkot.

The Nawáb, who had been kept in a species of confinement by his mother and Cháitibú and their unworthy favourites, now saw his opportunity to escape from the degrading tutelage in which he had been kept, and he wrote secretly to Colonel Barr, then Political Agent, to protect him from the indignities which he was suffering. Colonel Barr sent his assistant Captain Elliott to Júnágadh to make inquiries, but that officer died shortly after his arrival there, and was succeeded by Mr. Coulson of the Civil Service. When Mr. Coulson was camped at Wanthali, the Nawáb delighted at seeing an end to all the miseries he had been enduring, contrived to elude the vigilance of his mother and Cháitibú, and in company with his brother-in-law Shekh Bahá-úd-din escaped to Wanthali and threw himself upon Mr. Coulson's protection, which that officer gladly afforded him. Mr. Coulson reported what had occurred to Colonel Barr, who also was delighted to see the Nawáb freed from the domination of the set of intriguers who had hitherto conducted affairs, and he ordered Mr. Coulson to proceed to Júnágadh and see that the ladies in question were no longer allowed to remain against the will of the Nawáb in his own palace. While the Nawáb was at Wanthali he was joined by all the respectable men of the State, such as Khán Bahádúr Sále Hindi, C.I.E., Jamál Khán, and others who were opposed to the intrigues of the queen-mother and her low confederates. Eventually Colonel Barr came in person to Wanthali, and brought the Nawáb back to Júnágadh and acted with such firmness, tact, and judgment, that the Nawáb Sáhib was installed in his palace, and the intriguers expelled without either bloodshed or disturbance. In all the affairs of the time Colonel Barr was ably seconded by his Assistant Mr. Coulson. In the meantime Keshavji obtained the assistance of Mr. Connon, who came up to Rájkot as his counsel to procure his release from confinement, and he printed many articles regarding Júnágadh affairs in the papers. The Bombay Government however did not approve of Colonel Barr's action, and removed that officer, and Colonel (then Major) Anderson was appointed Acting Political Agent until the arrival of Colonel (then Major) Keatinge, *V.C.*, C.S.I., who was permanently appointed to the post, and officers were deputed to Júnágadh to inquire whether any pressure had been put on the Nawáb to change his ministers, that is to say, to get free from Keshavji and the queen-mother and her vicious confederates. The Nawáb, who was much alarmed lest he should be again put under their degrading influence, remonstrated strongly, and was eventually permitted to remain his own master. Keshavji and his two companions were tried and found guilty and sentenced, Keshavji to ten years' imprisonment and his two companions to nine years each. Keshavji died in 1871, only two months after his release from confinement. Virji had died previously, having fallen from a window in the Úparkot, where he had been placed in confinement for instigating the queen-mother to rebel. Nawáb Sáhib Mahabat Khánji in February 1870 attended the darbár held in Bombay by Sir Seymour Fitzgerald in honour of the Duke of Edinburgh, and in November 1872 visited Bombay, and attended the durbár held there by Lord Northbrook on the occasion of the bestowal of the rank of G.C.S.I. on the Begum of Bhopál, and again went to Bombay in October 1874, and paid his respects to H. R. H. the Prince of Wales, and attended the darbár held on that occasion. He also attended the Imperial Darbár at Delhi, on the 1st of January 1877, and availed himself of this opportunity to visit Ágrá, Cawnpore, Lucknow, Banáras, Calcutta, Alláhábád, and other towns and places of interest. The Nawáb's personal salute was increased on the occasion of the Delhi Darbár from 11 to 15 guns. He had also visited Rájkot on six occasions, namely in the years 1859, 1866, 1869, 1870, 1871, and 1874. During 1878 Ráo Bahádúr Gokalji Jhálá, who had for many years been minister of the State, died, and Khán Bahádúr Jamádár Sale Hindi, C.I.E., succeeded him in the office of Diwán. Prince Bahádúr Khanji, the recognized heir to the gádi, has been educated for about two years at the Rájkúmár College at Rájkot, and has travelled in India with Colonel Lester in 1873-74, and when the Nawáb Sáhib was absent from Júnágadh in 1876-77 on his visit to Delhi, Bahádúr Khánji acted for his father at Júnágadh, and conducted affairs in a satisfactory manner. The principal persons at the late Nawáb Sáhib's Court were—(1) Vazir Bahá-úd-din, his brother-in-law; (2) Khán Bahádúr Jamádár Sále Hindi, C.I.E., Chief Minister; (3) Ázam Narsingh Parsád; (4) Ázam Nihálchand; (5) Jamádár Muhammad Abu Panch; (6) Jamádár Mubárak; (7) Jamádár Syad bin Násir; (8) Jamádár Jamálbhái; (9) Jamádár Jamál Khán; (10) Treasurer Ismáil Shet; (11) Jamádár Muhammad bin Farid Khán, in charge of the State jewels; (12) Jamádár Muhammad Pirbhái, the head of the forces, and many others. Since the above was written, H. H. Nawáb Sáhib Mahábat Khánji, K. C. S. I., departed this life on the 29th September 1882, and has been succeeded by his son, Prince Bahádúr Khánji, who is now the Nawáb Sáhib of Júnágadh.

CHAPTER IV.

DETAILS OF ADMINISTRATION.

LAND.

Land Tenure—Khálsáh and Bárkháli land.

There are two principal divisions in the land tenures of the State of Júnágadh, namely (1) the Khálsáh and (2) the Bárkháli or lands held by vassals and others. The Khálsáh land is held on four different tenures, viz. (1) Bhogvero, or payment of certain cash dues in addition to a share in kind; (2) Vighoti, where a certain assessment is made per vighá for a fixed period of years; (3) Udhad, where a fixed sum is levied for a certain number of years, agreed on; (4) Bhágwatái, where a share in the produce in kind only is taken, and where cash dues are not levied.

Pasáitá, Dharmádá, Jivái, Inámi, Patel Palat, and Service tenures.

The Pasáitá land is land held rent free of the State on condition of village police service. Dharmádá, or tenure by religious service, includes lands bestowed on ascetics or holy men of whatever religion, as well as grants in endowment of mosques, temples, &c. Jivái includes lands granted for maintenance as well as purely service tenures. The Inámi tenure differs from the others in this, that no service can be demanded from the tenant. Patel Palat consists of land granted rent free to Patels in consideration of their services, and instead of pecuniary remuneration.

Kapál grás. Múlgrás.

Kapál grás is land bestowed in apanage onc adets of the house. Múlgrás for the purposes of the Rájasthánik Court, has been defined by Government in a Notification published in the *Bombay Government Gazette*, dated Bombay Castle, August 26th,

1873; further discussion regarding this tenure is therefore here unnecessary.

Tenant-proprietors under the State.

Land held on the Bhogvero tenure pays a plough tax in cash varying from Rupees eight to Rupees forty per sánti, the sánti varying from 3C to 75 vighás. The Rájbhág or State share of the produce under this tenure is from one-eighth to one-fourth in rain crops, and from one-seventh to one-sixth in irrigated crops. Land held on the vighoti tenure is assessed at rates differing according to the quality of the land, and the amount levied on rain-crop land varies from koris 4 to koris 8 per vighá, and on irrigated land from 12 koris to 15 koris per vighá.

For sugar-cane there is a special rate, viz., 40 to 50 koris per vighá.

The tenant has no power to sublet or transfer his holding, this transference being made by the State alone, which on such occasions levies a royalty consisting of a sum of ready money called Kasumbo from the incoming tenant.

The tenant is theoretically a tenant at will, but the State from motives of self-interest as well as prescription rarely terminates a tenure.

Tenant-proprietors under the vassals.

In vassal hold villages the Bhágwatái system is universal, and the grásiás' share of the produce is about the same as that levied by the Darbár. Tenants as a rule are better off in State villages, as the supervision of the grásiá is more minute than that of the Darbári official, he has more masters also in a grásiá village and is more liable to veth.

Land whether or not liable to debt.

No land is liable to be sold by orders of any Civil Court in payment of a cultivator's private debts, indeed as the land does not belong to him, it naturally is not liable to sale on account of his liabilities. The cultivator's cattle and implements of husbandry are specially exempted from sale by order of any Civil Court.

The revenue is collected in both crown and vassal villages at the time the grain is brought to the village grain-yards, that is to say for rain crops, excepting cotton, in November and December, and for cotton, wheat, gram, &c., in March and April. The amount due to the State is either fix on the principle above described, or by the dhál or kaltar system whereby a guess is made from the standing crop, and a fixed quantity settled as payable to the State. This latter custom obtains also sometimes in vassal villages.

Land revenue how collected.

Arrears of land revenue rarely occur, but where arrears may exist, they are enforced by mohsals and should these fail to procure payment, the property of the cultivator (his cattle and implements of husbandry alone excepted) is sold to satisfy the State demand. Such cases as a rule only exist where advances have been made by the State to the ryot to buy seed or cattle, or other necessary expenditure.

Collection of arrears how enforced.

Justice.

The constitution of Courts for the Civil and Criminal administration of justice in the Júnágadh State is as follows :—

There are in all 32 Criminal and 26 Civil Courts.

Out of 32 Criminal Courts, 29 are of Magistrates, viz., 16 exercises powers of 15 days' imprisonment of either description and 50 kories fine; 12 have powers of imprisonment of either description up to 6 months and fine up to 500 kories of their own motion, and can give sentences to double this extent with the sanction of the District Court, to which Court they commit cases beyond their cognizance; one at the capital has powers of imprisonment of either description up to one year and fine up to 1,000 koris, and double this extent with the sanction of the District Court.

Criminal Courts.

Then comes the Court of the Assistant District Judge, to which all cases, except those of murder and dacoity, are committed by subordinate 1st Class Magistrates. He has powers of imprisonment of his own motion up to 5 years and fine up to any extent, and up to 7 years' imprisonment with the sanction of the District Court. There are two District Judges' Courts, one at the capital and another at Bábriáwád. Judges of these Courts have powers of imprisonment of either description up to 14 years and fine to any extent, and also can pass a sentence of death, but to carry out that sentence the sanction of the Huzur Court has previously to be obtained through the Varisht (or Higher) Court.

Civil Courts.

There are 26 Courts of original civil jurisdiction with powers as under :—3 Wahiwatdárs' Courts with powers up to 100 koris, no appeal lies from their decisions; 1 Court of Small Causes at the capital with powers up to 500 koris, and its decisions are appealable to the Varisht Court alone; 14 with powers up to 2,000 koris; and 5 with 10,000 koris; and 1 up to 20,000 koris (Babriáwád District Judge's Court), and 1 up to lakh koris (Assistant District Judge's Court at Júnágadh). The chief Civil Court at the capital, viz., that of District Judge, can entertain civil claims up to any amount.

It should be observed that of these Courts, 11 are purely Criminal, 5 purely Civil, and 21 exercise both Civil and Criminal jurisdiction.

Appellate Courts.

There are two Courts of first appeal, viz. (1) that of District Judge at Júnágadh, and (2) that of Bábriáwád. They hear appeals from the decisions of their respective subordinate Courts. Then comes the Varisht (or Higher) Court; it hears appeals from the decisions of District Courts and has powers of reference, revision, and supervision. The final Court of Appeal is called the Huzur Court, where His Highness, with the assistance of his two ministers, decides appeals from the decisions of the Varisht Court.

Working of the Courts.

The working of the Criminal Courts is on the whole satisfactory. There is much delay and much confinement on mere suspicion and without perhaps adequate cause, but this though shocking to

English lawyers, excites no complaint in a country where the ryot is accustomed to be imprisoned at the will of his superior; and but few guilty persons escape. The sentences inflicted are usually milder than those in regulation districts, and the system admirably suits the governed. In the Civil Courts here as elsewhere, the record is usually insufficiently clear, and the tendency to amalgamate proceedings and judgment into one rambling decision exists here as elsewhere, but on the whole substantial equity is administered and the Courts are yearly improving, and during the last few years much attention has been given to the subject of lessening the delay in both Civil and Criminal cases.

There are also twenty-four other departments of State, namely the Diván's daftar, the Múlki daftar, the Rájwári daftar, the Hisábi daftar, the Daftari daftar, the Heir-Apparent's daftar, the Toshákhánah, the Bháyáti daftar, the Survey Department, the Rájprakarni daftar, the Bakhshi daftar, the English department, the Educational department, the Attachment department, the Registration department, the Police department, the Jail department, the Guest, accommodation, the Small-pox establishment, the Postal department, the Printing establishment, the Customs department, the Municipal department, and the Pound Fund office.

Miscellaneous Departments.

Most of these require no explanation, but the Diwán's daftar is that of the Chief Minister. The Múlki is the Revenue department, the Rájwári is the Political department, the Hisábi is the Account department, and the Daftari daftar is the one which issues grants and State deeds; the Toshákhánah is the Treasury; the Bháyati daftar is concerned with the affairs of cadets of the house and Múlgrásiás; the Rájprakarni department transacts affairs of holders of estates in maintenance; and the Bakhshi department enlists and dismisses sipáhis and pays them, &c.

Internal management of vassal villages.

The usual mode of internal management in vassal villages closely resembles the English manorial holdings. The Gámáit land corresponds to the tenemental land and the Gharkhed to the demesne lands; where there are more landholders than one, and when a complete separation of interests has not been effected, it is usual for each shareholder to have separate Gharkhoḍ (demesne lands) while the tenemental lands remain joint amongst all the shareholders, the produce being divided according to the position of each in the family.

Incidence of the land tax.

A revenue survey is in progress, and in a few years the whole area of the State will be surveyed. The classing of lands is principally done by local officials who are acquainted both with the land and with the former assessments. The rates at present levied are approximately as follows :—

Crops.	Rate levied per Acre.		
	Good land.	Middling land.	Indifferent land.
	Rs.	Rs.	Rs.
Sugarcane...............	45	30	...
Wheat	18	12	...
Tobacco	10	6	3
Bájri	10	6½	3
Jowár	8	4	1½
Cotton	10	5	1½

The assessment is collected by two instalments, viz., the first on Mágsar súd 2nd, and the second on Waishákh súd 2nd. Remissions are granted in all vighoti villages on good cause being shown, and even in Bhágwatái villages, if for instance a cultivator's cattle were to die, a remission would be granted from the vero or ready money levies, to enable him to buy others.

State demand how levied.

The different Mahāls, which formerly used to be farmed out to influential persons of the Court are now directly administered by an official styled a Wahiwatdár, who corresponds to the Tahsildar of Northern India, and who receives monthly pay and is immediately responsible to the Darbár.

Police and Military.

The village police consists of a Múkhi, or Police Patel aided by the village pasáitás. Besides this the tálukah police are divided into five sections and are quartered in five distinct stations under the orders of five Assistant Superintendents of Police. The supreme control of the police is exercised by the Police Superintendent. In addition to these, police are stationed at different posts throughout the State under the control of Police Foujdárs who are subordinate to the Assistant Superintendents. There are but few pagis or trackers in Sorath, though in important villages some are usually to be found. In many villages either Pasáitás or Jamádárs undertake police duties, and are responsible for compensation in case of thefts or robberies.

Military Force.

The military force under Júnágadh consists of 275 drilled horsemen, 125 drilled footmen, 30 drilled artillerymen, and 13 guns, not including those mounted in forts, &c. In addition to these there are about 1,000 horsemen and about 6,000 (sibandi) footmen.

Revenue and Finance.

In the year 1876 the gross revenue of the State amounted to koris 63,60,312-10-0 or about Rs. 18,17,233-2-10 equivalent to about £1,81,723, derived from the following sources :—

Abstract of ordinary Revenue of the Júnágadh State for 1876.

Source of Revenue.	Amount Realized.			
	Rs.	a.	p.	£
Net Land Revenue	12,12,587	15	9	121,258¾
Sea Customs	1,42,189	10	0	14,219
Land Customs	1,78,525	4	9	17,852½
Salt	19,164	3	6	1,916½
Opium	14,434	3	5	1,443½
Liquor Licenses	4,112	0	10	411¼
State Dues and Taxes	27,145	9	7	2,714½
Stamps, Fees and Fines	33,140	2	7	3,314
Interest on Government Securities	....			.....
Miscellaneous	99,177	9	0	9,917¾
*Zortalabi	86,755	7	5	8,675½
Total of Ordinary Revenue...	18,17,232	2	10	181,723¼

* This must not be considered as a fixed amount, as several items are yet in dispute.

The entire amount of tribute and similar demands paid annually by the State of Júnágadh through the British Government are as follows :—

Details of Tribute.

		Rs. a. p.
Tribute—Peshwá's share.	28,394	
„ Gáekwár's „	42,210	70,852 0 0
To Gáekwár on account of Bábáriáwár......	248	
Payments to the Jetpúr Káthis awarded at the time of the separation of rights		1,522 13 1
Payments to Jáfarábád, Gondal, and Porbandar on account of certain villages		12,406 3 3
Grand Total...Rs.		84,781 0 4
or about ......£		8,478 2 0

Ordinary expenditure.

The ordinary expenditure of the State,—including Rs. 1,12,850-0-8 on establishments, tribute, &c., as above, village improvements Rs. 1,42,812-7-4, public works 1,70,140-1-3,—amounted in A.D. 1876 to Rs. 15,84,387-4-6; but this amount was in excess of the ordinary amount owing to H. H. the Nawáb's visit to Bombay to meet H. R. H. the Prince of Wales, and the marriage of then Heir-Apparent Bahádúr Khánji to a daughter of the Heir to the Bálásinor gádi. In ordinary years the average expenditure is about Rs. 12,00,000.

Surplus how invested.

The annual surplus is deposited in the Toshákhánáh, but the Nawáb Sáhib, like most native Chiefs, is unwilling to disclose the actual amount in his Treasury, consequently the exact figures are not furnished, but report supposes the amount to be about 50 lákhs.

Customs and Transit Dues.

Sea Customs—Export dues.

The Júnágadh ports are not recognized as British Indian ports. The principal export duties are those on cotton, wool, ghi, oil-seeds and grain as under :—On cotton an *ad valorem* duty of 2 per cent. plus 1 anna per kori at Veráwal and Rs. 1½ at Bherái per bale of 20 maunds. 2½ per cent. is levied at the remaining ports. On all other exports a 2 per cent. *ad valorem* duty plus 1 anna per kori is levied at Verával, $2\frac{1}{2}$ per cent. at other ports excepting Bherái, where one per cent. is levied.

Sea Customs—Import dues.

The Import dues are levied at the same rates as the export dues at the ports mentioned.

Land Customs—Export and Import dues.

Land customs are levied in the Júnágadh territory at $4\frac{1}{2}$ per cent. *ad valorem*, both export and import.

Miscellaneous Cesses.

Fruit-tree tax.

The fruit-tree tax is one of the more important taxes. From all old mango and other fruit-trees one-fourth of the yearly yield is taken, but now a tax is being substituted of Re. 1 per tree per annum from the date it begins to bear. Until a tree bears a crop of about 50 mangoes it is not considered to be taxable. On gúndá trees 8 annas is levied per tree. On cocoanut trees $2\frac{1}{2}$ annas per tree are levied.

Grazing Fees.

Grazing fees (mákhni) are levied at the following rates:—

Animal.	Amount.	Remarks.
Goat	$\frac{1}{16}$ of a kori per annum	No reduction is allowed for flocks.
Sheep	$\frac{1}{16}$ of a kori per annum	
Cow	$\frac{1}{4}$ of a kori per annum	
Bullock	$\frac{1}{2}$ of a kori per annum	
Buffalo	$\frac{1}{8}$ of a kori per annum	
Camel	$\frac{4}{4}$ of a kori per annum	
Calves of Cows	$\frac{1}{16}$ to $\frac{1}{8}$ of a kori according to size.	
Calves of Buffaloes.	$\frac{1}{8}$ to $\frac{1}{4}$ of a kori according to size.	

These taxes are paid by Rabáris, Bharwáḍs, Chárans, and other professional graziers.

Taxes on handicrafts and labourers.

Úbhaḍ vero or a tax levied from the labouring classes is taken at the rate of 1 to 5 koris per house according to the number of persons. Kasab vero is generally levied at the rate of from 1 to 10 koris per house of artizans according to the number of persons. In certain mahále a fixed sum is levied per caste, the actual amounts payable from each house being collected by the caste Patel.

Postal arrangements.

The Government Postal arrangements are under the charge of the Inspecting Postmaster, Kachh and Káthiáwár, but the State also maintains five lines of local post, viz. (1) from Júnágadh to Úná viâ Máliá and Veráwal; (2) Júnágadh to Kútiáná viâ Wanthaliá, (3) Júnágadh to Visáwadar; (4) Júnágadh to Jetpúr viâ Wadál; (5) Júnágadh to Bagaḍú viâ Khaḍia. The total expenditure on these lines in 1876 was Rs. 2,046-13-8 and the income was Rs. 3,748, thus affording the State a net income of Rs. 1,701-2-4. The advantages this post offers over the Government post are two—(1) letters reach sooner and (2) the cost of stamps is less. Thus a ticket costing one-sixth of a kori only is affixed to letters of half a tolá, the fee for registration being ¼ kori. As, roughly speaking, 8½ koris are equivalent to one rupee, it will be seen that the cost of stamps is very small.

Education.

According to the census of 1881, 10·528 per cent. of the total Hindú male population, including Jains, were able to read and write or were under instruction, ·019 per cent. of the Hindú female population, including Jains, were sufficiently educated to be able to read or write or were under instruction, 13·395 per cent. of the total Músalmán male population could read and write or under instruction, while ·017 per cent. of Músalmán females could read and write or were prosecuting their studies.

The following table will show the number of State Schools:—

Name of School.	Number.	Remarks.
High School......	1	
Vernacular Schools on Fund......	66	
Do. do. not on Fund......	3	
Girls' Schools on Fund......	4	
Do. not on Fund......	4	
Úrdú Schools......	1	
Sanskrit Schools......	1	
Total......	80	

A cadet of the Júnágadh House, Edal Khánji by name, is prosecuting his studies at the Rájkúmár College at Rájkot.

Sanitary.

There are 8 dispensaries in this State, costing altogether Rs. 21,875 in A. D. 1883. They are situated at Júnágadh, Veráwal, Pátan, Kûtiáná, Úná, Máliá, Bagdû and Wanthali. The Júnágadh dispensary is a very good one, and there is a fine hospital in that town superintended by Mr. Amidás Manji, L.M. In this hospital also an appointment of a midwife has recently been made by the State. At the end of 1883, 13,471 patients were treated in the Júnágadh hospital.

Public Works.

The department of Public Works has been placed under a Native Engineer, who has served under the Agency Engineer. This man's name is Kánji Makanji, and he receives a salary of Rs. 300 per mensem. Considerable progress has been made in the construction of roads and public buildings. The city of Júnágadh will soon be completely transformed, in consequence of the handsome buildings which are everywhere springing up, and the care and taste which have been displayed in the formation of gardens in the suburbs. The High School, which was opened in A. D. 1881, is a handsome substantial building in a central and airy situation. A new jail, capable of accommodating 300 prisoners, is now nearly completed. The site has been well chosen, and is in the vicinity of the Military lines, which will completely command the interior. Dharmashálás for the convenience of travellers have been built at the North, South, and West Gates at the expense of the State: large and handsome additions are being made to the palace; the streets of the Bazár are being widened and provided with a uniform frontage of cut-stone, and a large drainage scheme has been set on foot. Similar activity has been shown in the districts. The road from Júnágadh to Veráwal, 56 miles in length, is now complete, with the exception of one bridge, and is in good working order. Commodious Dharmashálás have been provided on this line by communication for the convenience of travellers. A very nice Travellers' Bangalow, with every accomodation, having been constructed at Kesod, is useful for Europeans. A first-class road is constructed between the capital and the railway terminus at Dhoráji, and the work on the Droráji-Porbandar road within the State limits is in a very forward state. The lines for the Troops and Police are in the immediate vicinity of the new jail and are well constructed substantial buildings. The main roads running through the State, viz., from Júnágadh towards Jetpúr and Dhoráji, from Júnágadh to Veráwal, from Pátan to Práchi, a place of Hindú pilgrimage, is under construction; and in the portions of Júnágadh territory between Jetpúr and Porbandar are finished with the exceptions of bridges over the Ozat and the Venu rivers. The bridge over the latter is being constructed. Several other handsome buildings have been constructed at the capital, such as the Máhábat circle, the Court House, Hospital, and State Bangalow. The magnificent Sardár Taláo has been cleaned out and bunded. A Mausoleum and Musjid in memory of His Highness the late Nawáb Sáheb Sir Mahábat Khánji, K. C. S. I., are being constructed at a very large expense.

Forests and Tree Planting.

The great natural forest in the Júnágadh State is called the Gir, and is about 50 miles long by 20 to 25 miles in breadth. It abounds in useful timber, but owing to the little care taken of it no large timber has been hitherto grown there. But the Nawáb is now anxious to preserve this fine forest and grow timber. It abounds in teak, sissoo, sájar, beḍá, and other useful woods, and bamboos abound in places though of a smaller kind than those which are found in the forests of Gújarát. There is also a fine forest in the Girnár clump of hills near Júnágadh. The lion is still to be found in the Gir, but is getting very rare. No efforts have yet been made towards planting fruit or timber trees on a large scale.

---

j

CHAPTER V.

TOWNS AND PLACES OF INTEREST.

Number.	Name of Town or Village.	Page	Number.	Name of Town or Village.	Page
1	Bagasrá	74	25	Lodhwá	123
2	Bálágám	76	26	Majevadi	124
3	Bhandûri	77	27	Máliá	124
4	Bhensán	77	28	Mángrol	127
5	Bherái	78	29	Nágasri	131
6	Bhûwátimbi	78	30	Pasnávadá	132
7	Bhûwáwádá	79	31	Pátan	137
8	Chhelná	80	32	Phûlká	133
9	Chitrod (see under Verát)	150	33	Práchi Kûnd	132
10	Chorwád	80	34	Rámpúrá	134
11	Dátráná	81	35	Ránpúr	134
12	Delwáḍá (see under Uná)	148	36	Rohisá	135
13	Devdá	83	37	Sháná Caves	136
14	Dhámlej	83	38	Sásan	137
15	Dhandhûsar	84	39	Sil (see under Bagasrá)	74
16	Gádhakḍá	85	40	Somnáth	137
17	Girnar	86	41	Sûtrápádá	144
18	Gorakhmadhi	91	42	Ṭûlsisháma	147
19	Júnágadh	92	43	Úná	148
20	Kankái (see under Verát)	150	44	Vejalkothá	149
21	Kesod	117	45	Verát	150
22	Khorásá	118	46	Veráwal	152
23	Koili	119	47	Visáwadar	153
24	Kûtiyáná	120	48	Wanthali	155

SIL-BAGASRÁ.

These two towns are taken together because they were the holding granted to the Ráizádahs when their power and estate in Júnágadh was confiscated in the reign of the Emperor Akbar, and though Sil is about fifteen miles from Bagasrá, they are for this reason always spoken of together. Sil is on the sea-coast, about six miles N. W. of Mángarol. Bagasrá is about thirteen miles N. N. W. of Sil and is about four miles from the sea-shore. The population of Sil was 1,178, and that of Bagasrá 4,830 by the census of 1872, but they were terribly affected by the famine of 1878-79. In 1881 the population of Sil fell to 929 and Bagasra to 1,711 souls. The Sil creek is very good and would be well fitted for navigation, but its mouth gets blocked up with sand, and is thus rendered useless or nearly so. It seems capable of much improvement. Ráizádahs still hold land in the Sil and Bagasrá villages. Ráizádah was the name given by the Múhammadans to the descendants of Rá Mandlik, who received this estate in jágir. Former cadets are called Chûḍásamas, Sarvaiyás, &c., but Ráizádahs are only the descendants of Rá Mandlik. Bagasra lies thirty-four miles to the South-West of Júnágadh and thirteen miles N. N. W. in a straight line from Sil, though the distance between them by road is sixteen miles. Formerly a separate Wahiwatdár or Revenue official resided here, but now it forms a sub-division of the Sil Mahál. It appears from the inscription in the temple of the Koteshwar Máhádeva at Kodinár that in $\frac{\text{St. } 1328}{\text{A. D. } 1272}$ this village was under the rule of Visaldeva Wághelá, the Rájá of Anhilwárá Pátan, the then lord paramount of Gûjarát, and that he granted it to dependant of his, named Náná, a Nágar Bráhman, who also held a seventh share in the revenue of Mángarol. There is also a very interesting pályá or funeral monument in the grainyard at Bagasrá, dated $\frac{\text{St. } 1448}{\text{A. D. } 1392}$, from which it seems that Palo, son of Sámo, was slain in battle at Bagasrá in the victorious reign of Shri Mokalsingh. This is the Chûḍásama Ráo of Júnágadh. Later pályás bear the names of the Ahmadabad Sultáns as being lords paramount here. All these pályás bear the name Bagasrá. Afterwards in $\frac{\text{St. } 1528}{\text{A. D. } 1472}$ the Bagasrá Chovisi was granted in jágir to Bhûpatsingh, son of Ráo Mandlik, the last Rajpût ruler in Júnágadh. The descendants of this Bhûpatsingh, who are called Ráizádahs, are still living in certain villages of the Kesod Mahál. The village lands form part of the huge marsh called the Ghed, and are inundated in the rainy season. Kása grass grows spontaneously in the Ghed, the green grass is cut and given to cattle to eat, when the grass seeds, the seed or grain is collected and called Kasaiyá and is eaten by the residence of the Ghed villages. As it is not considered a grain, it is eaten by Hindus on fast days. This grass has bulbous roots, and the bulbs are black and the size of small potatoes. They are also cut up and the husk removed, and then boiled and eaten. These bulbs are called Lodh when green, and Bid when dry. Thegi *Cyperus Jemenicus*, a sedge, is also found in the Ghed and in the sand-hills on the sea-coast. There are thousands of lotus plants in the Ghed. The pods of the lotus are called Kûmnás, and they contain small white seeds, which are made into bread and eaten by the poorer classes and also by the rich on fast days. The gram grown in the Ghed is specially famous both for its excellent flavour and because it is very easily cooked. It is called "ghedia chaná" or ghedia gram. The population of Bagasrá consists chiefly of Mehars, Ghedia Kolis, Mehmans, Khojahs, Lohánás, Girnárá Bráhmans, Sindhis, &c.

BÁLÁGAUM.

Formerly in Mûhammadan times, this village was called Ghebanpûr, and was almost entirely inhabited by Mûhammadans, but afterwards falling waste it was repopulated by a Sorathia Áhir named Bálwa, and after him has been called Bálágaum; but others say that it is called Bálágaum because built on a lofty site. There is here a sect of Márgi Sádhús, who consider one Dásá Báwá, an ascetic of the Sagar tribe of Áhirs, as their religious precepter. These people are called Dásá panthis. Dásá is said to have gone once to bathe in the village well and to have subsequently been seen no more, and his worshippers consider that he was caught up into heaven. His turban was found on the steps of the well and is still adored by his followers. About a mile to the east of the village is the temple of Wásang Devi, the tutelary goddess of the Joshipûrá tribe of Wadnagará Nágars. There is a Government vernacular school here. Bálágaum forms a separate revenue sub-division under Júnágadh. The village lies about twenty-four miles to the W. S. W. of that city. A revenue officer and a 2nd Class Magistrate have their head-quaters here. The population of Bálágaum, according to the census of 1872, was 2,923, but diminished to 2,858 souls after the famine of 1878-79.

Bhandúri.

Bhandûri, a large village with a population of 981 souls according to the census of 1872, which increased in 1,881 to 1,095, is situated on the Júnágadh Verāwal trunk road at a distance of about thirty-eight miles from Júnágadh and eighteen miles from Verāwal. It is the head-quarters of the mahál of that name, and a Wahiwatdár and a 2nd Class Magistrate reside there. There is no outer town wall, but an inner citadel which has a picturesque appearance. The sugar-cane of this part of the country is particularly good.

Bhensán.

Bhensán is about twenty-four miles distant by the road from Júnágadh. It lies to the east of this town on the bank of the Úben, which river rises in a rising ground called the Úbenio Timbo, about three miles to the east of the village. Formerly this village was a nes or hamlet, and some Rájpûts of Rib or Ribrá who had lost their buffaloes, found them here. They then took up their residence here, and from the fact of having recovered their buffaloes at this place, called the hamlet Bhensán. It is now the head-quarters of a Mahál, and a Wahiwatdár and 1st Class Magistrate reside here. The population consists principally of Wániás, Bráhmans, Lohánás and Kanbis, and according to the census of 1872 consisted of 3,029 souls, but this number fell to 1,631 in 1881 after the famine of 1878-79. The cotton of the Bhensán district is considered to be of good quality. In a Valabhi copper-plate, found at Timbdi near Bhensán, mention is made of a village called Bhasant, which possibly may be an ancient name of Bhensán. Formerly a local ascetic named Devidás resided here, who had such miraculous powers that to this day he is called Satya Devidás. His shrine is about two miles from Bhensán to the north-west. A fair is held here on the 2nd of the light half of the month of Áshádh, and the Báwá distributes a meal to the people gathered. All eat together without distinction of caste, Hindús and Musalmáns together, but the Dhedhs dine separately. They drink water, too, from one and the same trough. It is said that lepers are cured by the sanctity of this place, and hence many come to reside here. The village was attacked and plundered by one Hamir Mehar about fifty years ago, but is now again populous. There is a Government vernacular school here.

Bherái.

Bherái is situated on a branch of the Devrápûri creek called Dúkhden (or trouble giving) from its numerous windings. The Darbár are excavating a straight channel to connect Bherái with the Devrápûri creek. This channel is to be called, when finished, Súkhden, or ease giving. Bherái trades pretty briskly during the cotton season, and is a rising town. It is twelve miles to the north-east of Jáfarábád as the crow flies, but more by the road, as the creek has to be avoided. The population, according to the census of 1872, was 841 souls, and increased to 1,171 in 1881. Much salt is made near this town, and pearls are occasionally found in the oysters of the creek. Bherái is said to have been populated about 200 years ago by one Sádúl Mámya of the Rám tribe of Áhirs. The oldest memorial-stones are dated 1687 corresponding to 1743 St. The waste site of Bherái is about 300 yards to the east of the present village. To the north of Bherái there is a quarry of excellent yellow stone resembling marble. There is also a large quantity of a light coloured soft clay called Bhutdo, which is largely used by natives for washing their hair; the special quality of this clay is that it leaves the hair soft, and not dry and hard as lime-juice, arithá, &c., do. At the close of the last century when there was much warfare with Bhávnagar on the Bábriáwár frontier, Jamádár Laving Jákhrá and Áhir Rám Hádo much distinguished themselves.

Bhúwátimbi.

This village lies about fourteen miles to the north-east of Sútrápádá. The population, according to the census of 1872, was 275 souls, but this number dwindled to 268 in 1881, consequent on the famine of 1878-79. The village is said to have been repeopled by Kárdiá Hamir of Sûtrápádá in A. D. 1839, and the population now consists principally of Kárdiá* Rájpûts of the Bárad, Mori, Jhankát, and Gohil tribes. But it was founded early in the fifteenth century by Rájá or Grásiá Bhûvad. Thus the tank is called the Bhûvad Taláo. And I gather from the Sanskrit inscription that the tank was excavated by Bái Wágti, daugher of Bái Magti, wife of Ráj Bharam of Bárad race, for the spiritual benefit of Shri Bhûvad, so probably Wágti was the widow of Bhûvad, who was doubtless a grásiá of some adjacent village. The inscription mentions that it was inscribed in $\frac{\text{Samwat 1457}}{\text{A.D. 1401}}$ in the victorious reign of Ráj Shri Shivgan. This Shivgan was probably a Wája ruler of Somnáth. His name occurs also in the inscription at Phûlká in the Úná Parganáh, the date of which is $\frac{\text{Samwat 1445}}{\text{A.D. 1389}}$ so that the two inscriptions clearly refer to the same Shivgan. In the village is a grove of Rávana Tád trees, or the branched variety of the Palmyra.

Bhúwáwádâ.

The population of this village is ascribed to Rájá Bhûvad of the Bhûatimbi inscription. The village lies about sixteen miles north-east of Sûtrápádá, and about three and a half miles to the north of Bhûatimbi. There are old monuments dating from St. 1400 to 1500 in its lands, which shows the village to be about the same date as Bhûwátimbi. In 1872 the entire population was 76 persons, but it was almost depopulated by the famine of 1878-79, and in 1881 the population had sunk to 17 souls. It has been re-populated on a new site by the name of Bahádûrpûrá. The buildings and ruins in the village lands, such as wávs or wells with steps, and the remains of a fort with gates, as well as the actual extent of the lands which amount to 100 sántis, equivalent to about 2,000 acres, show that it must once have been a large and populous village. The Memati stream joins the Sûrmat river about a mile from this village. The water of the Memati is very deliterious to health.

* Kárdiá means a Rájpût who subsists by labour, cultivation, or service. Kár as contrasted with grás and Kárdiá with grásiá. The literal meaning is tax-payer from kar a tax, and dewûn to give, as contrasted with the grásiá tenure.

Chhelná.

Chhelná is situated in about the centre of the Gir Forest, about eighteen to twenty miles south of Visáwadar, and twenty-two to twenty-six miles N. E. of Pátan. It originally belonged to the Harsúrka Káthis of Visáwadar. The water of Chhelná is very unhealthy, and causes the belly to swell and the spleen to become enlarged. The village is surrounded by a stone wall and had a population, according to the census of 1872, of only 150 souls, but increased in 1881 to 195. In former times when it was wished to get rid of any state prisoner, he was sent to Chhelná. Few, except Sidis or Kolis, can withstand the poisonous quality of the water, and consequently in a short time he died. The population of this part of the Gir consists principally of Sidis or Kolis. The Somat river rises near the Nagḍi Wáo in the Chhelná limits, and flows into the sea near Mûl Dwárká.

Chorwáḍ.

Chorwáḍ is about nine miles S. E. of Mángarol and thirteen miles N. W. of Veráwal, and lies on the coast of the Arabian Sea. It has been, since the earliest days, famous for its betel gardens, and the flavour of Chorwáḍ betel is supposed to be very superior, and it is largely exported not only inland but also by sea. Chorwáḍ was in ancient times a dependency of Mángarol. It is said to have derived its name from being a notorious haunt of pirates. There are some curious images here in a patch of jungle called the Jhúnd. In later times, *i.e.*, after the collapse of the Moghal power in the peninsula, it was seized on by the Ráizádahs, but we have no record of the exact date of such seizure; but Sanghji or Singhji, the Ráizádah grásiá of Chorwáḍ, took an active part in the intestine wars of the eighteenth century; but he was killed in the battle of Máliá, fought between him and Aliya Hátti, and his descendants were much embarrassed as to how they should defray the arrears of the soldiery. As Ráná Sûltánji of Porbandar was connected by marriage with the deceased Singhji, his relatives in A.D. 1787 entrusted the fort and town to him on condition that he should defray the demands of the sipáhis. The Káná agreed, and took possession of the town, and thence his commandant of this town captured Veráwal. This caused a general insurrection against the Nawab along the coast, and Sútrápádá also rebelled. But in the course of a short time Veráwal was recovered, and Chorwáḍ also was conquered in A. D. 1788. Mokáji, the chief Ráizádah grásiá, was permitted to retire with his family to Dhoraji on this occasion under the protection of Jáḍejá Kúmbhoji of Gondal. Since this date Chorwáḍ has been a khálsah (crown) domain of the Júnágadh State. The trade of Chorwáḍ is insignificant, it being merely a roadstead. The population, according to the census of A. D. 1872, was 2,818 souls, but this fell to 1,299 after the severe famine of 1878-79 The air of Chorwáḍ is considered favourable to invalids.

Dátráná.

This village belongs to the Wadál revenue sub-division of the Júnágadh State. It is twelve miles south of Júnágadh and twenty miles south of Wadál. It is famous as being the birth-place of the Cháran woman Nágbái, who cursed Rá Mandlik, the last Rájpût sovereign of Júnágadh, when he insulted the modesty of her son's wife. Her father's name was Harjog Dámo; he had no issue, but finally after much serving of holy men, he obtained one daughter Nágbái through the intercession of an ascetic named Hirágar. Harjog resided at Dhanphûlia, about six miles south-west of Júnágadh. Nágbái was married to Cháran Rávsûr Bhásûr. Her descendants are still to be found at Dátráná, and are called Gorviálá Chárans. There is a shrine and memorial-stone of Nágbái at Dátráná. It is said that Rá Mandlik was enamoured of her son Nágájan's wife Minbái. When any great man visits a Cháran's village, it is the custom of the Cháran women to approach him face to face with a tray containing red powder (Kankû) moistened with water and some raw rice. They then make the caste mark on his forehead with the Kankû and affix some rice to it; they then throw some of the grain or some flowers over him and bless him, and depart after cracking their fingers against their temples. This last is emblematic of the person so doing taking the misfortunes of the person in whose honour this is done, upon her. When Minbái approached Rá Mandlik to perform this ceremony, he turned away from her in another direction because he was unwilling to accept her blessing, as his doing so would make her sacred from his unlawful desires. On his thus turning away Minbái said to Nágbái, "The Rá turns away." Nágbái said, "Try him in another direction, as perhaps there may be some bad omen to him in receiving a blessing in that direction." She went in all four directions, but the Rá still turned away from her. She then said to Nágbái, "I have tried all four directions, but he still turns away." Nágbái replied, "You need not try any more; it is not Mandlik who turns, but the days of his good fortune which have turned away from him." Minbái then was going away, when Rá Mandlik placed his hand on her bosom. Minbái ran screaming to her mother-in-law, and complained of the insult the Rá had put on her. Nágbái then cursed him as follows :—

जाशे राहानी रीत, राहापणु रेशे नही ;
भमतो मागीश भीख (ते दी) मुं संभारिश मंडलीक.

The rule of the Ráo shall pass away, and your sovereignty shall last no longer.

As a wanderer you shall beg for alms and shall then remember me, oh Mandlik.

पडशे जुनानी पोळ, दामो कुंड देखिश नहि ;
रतन जाशे रोळ (ते दी) मुं संभारिश मंडलीक.

The gate of the ancient Fortress (Júnágadh) shall fall;
You shall see the Dámo Kûnda no more;
(You our) jewel shall be laid in the dust,
And then shall remember me, oh Mandlik.

About half a mile north of the village is the Godhmo Hill, so named because fabled to have once been the residence of a demon of this name. There are small shrines of the goddesses Gátrád and Khodiár on the summit of this hill much respected by Káthis and Chárans. The hill is composed of a kind of syenite, and is covered with Ráyan trees (Mimusops Hexandra), and it is said that if the berries of this tree be taken away for private consumption they keep good, but if taken away for sale, maggots at once appear in them. The population of Datráná, according to the census of 1872, was 1,421, but sank to 1,273 souls in 1881, consequent on the famine of 1878-79.

Devḍá.

This village is situated ten miles to the north-west of Kûtiáná. Formerly the population consisted of Ods, but now there are many other castes. The population, according to the census of 1872, was 1,407, but swelled to 1,441 in 1881. In A.D. 1780 there was a scarcity in the province, and Malik Mûhammad of Roghḍá, who at that time held the forts of Devḍá and Khágasri, collected a large number of Sindhis in these forts and plundered the country of Kûmbhoji of Gondal. Kûmbhoji complained to Diván Amarji, after vainly attempting to persuade the Sindhis to cease their raids. Diván Amarji, perceiving the importance of checking of these Sindhis, marched against them, and was joined by his brother Govindji from Kûtiáná. They cannonaded and took both forts, and the Sindhis fled during the night. Devḍá is situated on the eastern bank of the river Minsár. About a mile to the south of Devḍá is the meeting of the Bileshvari and Minsár rivers. The junction of these streams is called Triveni, and a temple of Hatkeshwar stands there. The town wall of Devḍá is built of loose stone, but the inner citadel is of masonry. A Government vernacular school is in the village. There is a poem written by the bards on the conquest of Devḍá by Amarji Diván.

Dhámlej.

This village lies eleven and a half miles south-east of Sûtrápádá. According to the census of 1872, its population amounted to 1,274 souls, but in 1881, after the great famine of 1878-79, it sunk to 1,129. Excellent salt is produced here, and so famous is Dhámlej for its salt, that foolish people are called *Dhámlei no Kácho* or ignorant of Dhámlej, *i.e.* without salt or wit. It is said that Dhámlej was populated by the Jhálá Ráná Dhamalji of Jámbû in ancient times, and that he named it after himself. The old site of Dhámlej was, however, deserted, and the present village built on a new site. Dhámlej is celebrated for a tank near to the west of the village called Vishnû Gayá. It is also called Chakra Tirth, as the Báwá who resides at the tank produces a Chakra or discus about a foot in length by about 5 inches in breadth; this though supposed to be of stone floats in the water. There is an interesting inscription in this reservoir, dated $\frac{\text{Samvat 1437}}{\text{A.D. 1381}}$, showing that it was repaired by a Porwád Wánio, named Karamshi, minister of Rájá Bharma of Wájá race. There is an old temple of Somnáth Mahádeva close to this Kûnd or reservoir and there is a symbol of Naleshwar Mahádeva in a cave about a quarter of a mile to the northwest of the village.

Dhandhúsar.

This village is said to derive its name from the celebrated Dhûndhali Mal, who is supposed to have resided here for some time and to have excavated and built up the tank which gives its name to the village. In all probability Dhandh or Dhandhû was merely a Mehar, as the name is not uncommon in that tribe. On the bank of the tank is a temple of Shiva in a more or less ruined condition also ascribed to Dhûndhali Mala, and said to have been built at the same time as the tank was excavated. There is also an ancient well at Dhandhûsar called the Hániwav, built by a princess of Wanthali named Háni through her minister Gadádhar in $\frac{\text{Samvat 1445}}{\text{A.D. 1389}}$ during the reign of Chûdásama Mokalsingh, son of Jayasing. In one of the niches of this well is an image of the Sheshasháyi Bhagwán or Vishnû, who is supposed to sleep on the Sheshnág, who is himself immersed in the water. The villagers consider this an image of Háni, and women who are unable to nurse, or the owners of cows who give a scanty supply of milk, make a vow to wash the statue in milk if their supply of milk be increased. The Dhedhs consider Háni to have been a Dhedh woman, and to have subsequently been deified and adore this image as that of their tutelary goddess, and the well as sacred to her. This well has no todas or pillars at the entrance. The grove of trees overhanging the well swarm with flying foxes (*pteropus edwardsi*) in thousands, and in no place in the entire province are there such numbers of these creatures. They are said to have always dwelt here. Báwá Piárah, whose monastery is at Júnágadh, is said to have resided some time at Dhandhûsar; afterwards it became waste, but was repopulated six or seven hundred years ago by Mehar Noghá Dosá Deoránia. It again fell waste in the famine of $\frac{\text{Samwat } 1847}{\text{A. D. } 1791}$, and was repopulated in $\frac{\text{Samwat } 1889}{\text{A. D. } 1833}$, when Mehar Áto of Derwán, aided by Miáná Ráná Changal, attacked the village. They were twice repulsed by the Dhandhûsar Mehar Bhimsi Arsi Thápliá, but succeeded on their third attack and plundered the village. Dhandhûsar lies about nine miles north-west of Júnágadh. The population of this village according to the census of 1872 was 1,679 souls, but this number sank to 1,634 in 1881, consequent on the famine of 1878-79.

GÁDHAKDÁ.

This village is the head of a sub-division of the revenue division of Bherái and a subordinate revenue officer resides here. It is about eighty-four miles east south-east of Júnágadh, and thirty-six miles north-east of Úná. The high road from Kûndlá to Mahûwá passes through its lands. It is about nine miles south-east of Kûndlá. The name is said to be derived from Gátra (body) and Gadá to bury, because Báwá Somnáth of Gorakhmadi buried himself alive here. The Káthis of Gádhakdá had carried off his cattle. The Báwá accordingly went to Gádhakdá and demanded their restoration, but the Káthis refused. After waiting for three or four days fasting he dug a grave and descended therein. On seeing this the Káthis remonstrated with him and offered to come to terms, but he replied, "When an ascetic has once entered the grave, he may not return." Then he cursed the Káthis and said that they would never be prosperous in future, and then caused himself to be buried alive under a banyán tree still called Somnáth no Wad. Chomlá Khumáṇ of Gádhakdá distinguished himself by recovering some cattle of Júnágadh villages from the Khasiás of the Bhávnagar village of Sedardá. The population of Gádhakdá was 2,370 by the census of 1872, but sank to 1,794 in 1881, consequent on the famine of 1878-79. The town is surrounded by a fort wall and the river Phuljhar flows close by. A celebrated local poet called Nágji Máháráj, an Audich Bráhman by caste, was born here. He is specially famous for his stanzas or Kûndlias, in which he prophesied the principal events of each year up to Samvat 1955, corresponding to A. D. 1899. His descendants make public the Kûndlia or stanzas for the year on the first day of the new year.

Girnár.

The Girnár hill has five principal peaks—(1) Ambá Mátá (or the Girnári goddess) which is crowned by the temple of that goddess; (2) Gorakhnáth, the highest of all, which is 3,666 feet above the sea; (3) the Oghaḍ Shikhara; (4) Gûrû Datátreya; and (5) Kálká's peak, which is even now supposed to be the resort of Aghoris or Mardikhors. But the Pûránas enumerate no less than twenty-one different peaks. The fortress and the remnant of the old palace of the Chûḍásamás is still standing. Girnár is sacred to the 22nd Jaina Tirthankar Nemináth, and there are many Jaina temples on the hill. Three famous Kûndas or reservoirs are called the Gao-Mûkhi, Hanûmán Dhárá, and Kamandal Kûnda respectively. The great rock called the Bhairava Jap forms a most picturesque object, and from this rock ascetics and others were wont to hurl themselves in the hopes of being born in a more favourable state of existence in a new life. At the foot of the hill at a little distance lies Wámansthali, the ancient capital, while Balisthán, the modern Bilkhá, lies immediately at its base. (1) The ancient name of the Girnár hill is Ujjayanta or Girwar, but not Revatáchal as is sometimes supposed. Revatachal is the name of the hill immediately over the Revati Kúnda. At the foot of this hill is the celebrated Ásoka stone with the inscriptions of Ásoka, Rûdra Dámá, and Skanda Gûpta; these are all described at length in Burgess's Antiquities of Kachh and Káthiáwár. A little further on is the Palásini bridge built by Sûndarji Shavji, the first native agent to the British Government in the Political Department in Káthiáwár.

The Jainas sometimes incorrectly apply the name Revatáchala to the Girnár.

The gate called Wágheswari leads to the Girnár. Just within this gate is the Rám Jharokha, which is a lodging house for pilgrims to the Girnár, and opposite to this rest-house is the Salát Wáo so called because constructed by saláts or stone-masons. Immediately outside the Wágheswari gate is the Wágheswari Taláo, in the centre of which there is a well so that when the tank dries up water is obtained from the well. When this tank overflows in the rainy season water is conveyed from it in a channel to the Dátár Taláo or tank at the foot of the Dátár hill. The temple of the Wágheswari Mátá lies in the Wágheswari hill to the right of the road to the Dámodarkûnda. The road up the hill then crosses the Pálásini river by the bridge built by Sundarji Shavji, the horse merchant and agent to the British Government in some of their first dealings with the Chiefs of Káthiáwar. Then comes the Dámodar Kûnda or reservoir so called in honor of Krishna who is called by this name because when a child his mother tied one end of a string round his stomach and the other end to a large stone-mortar used for bruising grain. Krishna, however, ran off with the mortar, which struck between two large arjuna trees *(terminalia arjuna)* and uprooted them. These trees were really gods or devtás who had been compelled by a curse to take the form of trees and were doomed to remain thus till Krishna should uproot them when they returned to their former god-like shape. Krishna is called Dámodar from "Dáma" string and "Udar" belly, alluding to the string with which his mother tied him. The water of this Kûnda is accounted very sacred The water has the property of dissolving bones and Hindus throw in it such portions of the bones of their relations which may be found in the ashes of the funeral pile. The Revati Kûnda is close to the Dámodar Kûnda. It is so called in memory of Revati—daughter of Rájá Revat. She married Baldeva, the brother of Krishna. Rájá Revat was the king of Dwárká, but after Revati's marriage he came and resided at Girnár, and the hill immediately over the Dámodar Kûnda is called Revatáchal. Near the Dámodar Kûnda is a great place of cremation of the Hindus. The Dámodar Kûnda is 275 feet long by 50 feet broad. After leaving the Wágheswari gate and temple and before reaching the Dámodar Kûnd the traveller passes the boulder of rock on which are engraved the inscriptions of Asoka, Rûdra Dámá and Skandh Gûpta. This boulder lies a few yards to the right of the road and a few hundred yards from the Wágheswari gate. Proceeding onwards towards the foot of the Girnár one passes to the left, what was, perhaps, the site of the famous Sûdarshan Taláo built originally by some unknown king, and repaired by Asoka and afterwards by Rûdra Dámá, and after him by Skandh Gûpta. But if this be *not* the spot, there can be no doubt that it was in the enclosure of the hills to the north of the Girnár mountain. Here the hills enclose like a circle a large basin, the only exit being the Sûvarnarekha river. A bund 300 yards long and fifty feet high here would enclose a four-sided figure, each side of which would be about one mile long. It would amply repay the Júnágadh Darbár to bund up this pass into the hills and again restore the lake, if only for irrigating the neighbouring country.

About a mile and a half from the Dámodar reservoir is the temple of Bhavnáth Máhádev, and a mile and a half from thence is the foot of the ascent of the hill. The temple of Bhavnáth is on the banks of one of the numerous streams called Sûvarna Rekhá. A fair is held here on the 12th, 13th, and 14th of the dark half of the month of Máhá, but the gathering commences from about the 9th.

The Mrigi Kûnda or reservoir is situated here, and the people bathe in the Kûnda at fair time. At the foot of the ascent of the hill is a well called Chaḍáni Wáv or well of the ascent. There is also here a large Dharamsálá built by Premchand Raichand, a Bombay merchant.

In an underground room in one of the cloisters of the great temple of Neminàth is a statue of Párasnáth, from the chin of which a drop of water is supposed to constantly drop, hence it is called the Amijhará Párasnáth or nectar dropping

Párasnáth. I have frequently seen this statue, but have never yet seen the drop on the chin, but probably this is owing to the scanty rainfall of recent years (1878 always excepted). There are six parabs or rest-houses on the ascent, viz. (1) the Chhodá Parab, (2) Chor Parab, (3) Dholi Parab, (4) Káli Parab, (5) Máli Parab, and (6) the Suvávḍi Parab, so called because a pregnant woman making the pilgrimage is said to have given birth to a child there.

On the top of the hill, which the Jains hold to be sacred to Neminátn the 22nd tirthankar, are several Jain temples, especially one of Neminâth. The temple of Ambá Mátá which crowns the first peak of the hill is much resorted to by newly married couples of the different sub-divisions of the Bráhman caste. The bride and bridegroom have their clothes tied together, and attended by their male and female relations, adore the Goddess and present cocoanuts and other offerings. This pilgrimage is supposed to procure for the married couple a long continuance of wedded bliss through the blessing of the Goddess.

After the Girnár, the Dátár, 2,779 feet high, is the finest hill of this group. The Dátár hill has near its summit a small shrine of Jamial Sháh, and the hill is generally held sacred by Múhammadans, but Rajpûts and the lower classes of Hindus also hold it in reverence. Jamial Sháh is said to have come from Thathá in Sindh, and to have been sent to Júnágadh by his spiritual preceptor Pir Patta in the reign of Rá Mandlik, and to have devoted himself to inculcating the tenets of the Múhammadan faith. The Chillah or chief shrine of the Dátár is at the bottom of the hill. The Dátár is supposed to have a beneficial effect on lepers who repair thither in considerable numbers. There are several interesting groups of Buddhist caves in the neighbourhood of Júnágadh, and an interesting fragment of a Kshatrapa inscription has lately been discovered in the caves near Báwá Piárah's Math. This inscription mentions Swámi Chashtana and Jaya-Dámá, and is inscribed by the great grandson of Swámi Chashtana and the grandson of Jaya-Dámá. In this inscription Júnágadh is called Girinagara. On a mound in the jungle are the ruins of some ancient brick building locally called the Lákhá Medi. These bricks are some of them nearly two feet in length and are of a very red colour.

The following list shows the different groups of Buddhist caves at Júnágadh and its vicinity:—

1. Khápra Kodiá.
2. Úparkot (inside the fort).
3. Báwá Piárah's Math.
4. Bakotá.
5. Shakrio Tímbo.
6. Pancheshwar (newly discovered).
7. Mátri.
8. Hothal—Padmíní near Pádariá.

The most famous streams issuing from the Girnár clump are—(1) the Sûvarnarekha, (2) the Gûdájhali, and (3) the Kálwo. Lions used to abound in this clump, but have not now been seen for several years. One of the last was shot by Major Russell in 1869. Panther, wild pig, and sámbar may still be found. The jungle on these hills is principally composed of teak and other forest trees which are now preserved by the Nawáb.

There are also the remains of caves at the Mái Gadechi, and an old Hindu temple which has been turned into a mosque. Over the door is an interesting Arabic inscription dated so far back as Súr San 685 = A. D. 1284, to the effect that the mosque was constructed by (Imád-ûl-háj wa-ûl-haramain Áfif-ûd-dúnya wa-ûd-din) Abûl Kásim bin Áli-al-Abrahi. This inscription is most valuable, as it shows (1) that the Súr San era was in use before A.H. 745 (*vide* Thomas's Prinsep, vol. II., page 171) and that previous to the conquest of Gújarát by Álagh Khán in the reign of Sûltán Alá-ûd-din Khiljy, a Múhammadan noble resided at the court of the Júnágadh chieftain as agent for the Múhammadan pilgrims to Makkah and Madinah. This temple, now transformed into a mosque, is said by the Jains to have been built by Sámprati Rájá, the grandson of Ásoka.

Without the city of Júnágadh at a distance of about a mile

and a half is a tank called the Pari Taláo lying in a south-westerly direction. The tank is built on all sides with masonry, and was recently repaired by Sheikh Báhá-ûd-din, the Vazir of His Highness the Nawáb. It is said that the fairies used formerly to come and bathe in this tank, and hence it was called the Pari Taláo. There are steps down to the water from the top of the wall, and there is also a place where cattle can be watered. The water of the Taláo is good and lasts all the year round. The tank is 258 feet in length by 250 feet in breadth. The depth of the water in November is about 13 feet.

On the road to Wanthali, about five miles from Júnágadh and four and a half miles from Wanthali, is the Khengár Wáv or well which never closes to yield water even in famine years. The well is much ruined, but must have been a most beautiful one when in repair. Even now the carving, which remains, is most delicate, and the proportions of the pillars, &c., very graceful. This well evidently originally contained an inscription, as there are two niches for an inscription on either side as one descends the steps to the water, but they have been removed, and it is not known what has become of them. The construction of this well is attributed to Ráo Khengár II., who reigned from about A. D. 1098-1125.

Gorakhmadhi.

Gorakhmadhi so called from Gorakshnáth (popularly Gorakhnáth) or the protector of the seven senses of sight, hearing, &c. He was a celebrated ascetic, and the founder of the sect of Kánphátá Jogis, whose head-quarters are at Gorakhmadhi, which is situated on the bank of the Sarasvati, about nine miles east of Pátan, and about six miles west of Práchi kûnd. Twice every day provisions are distributed freely to all who may ask for them. When the provisions are cooked, a servant of the Abbot's goes to the bank of the Sarasvati and calls twice with a loud voice, "Whoever is hungry, come; the Abbot's table is spread:" and to whomsoever comes he dispenses a meal. The Abbot of the Kánphátá Jogis is called Náthji, a title corresponding to "my lord" or literally lord, sir. There are images of Gorakhnáth and of his spiritual preceptor Machhendranáth in a cave. There are many legends regarding Gorakhnáth and his spiritual preceptor, and how Gorakhnáth surpassed his religious teacher in holiness, whence the Gûjaráti proverb गुरुपे चेला आगळा. The disciple hath surpassed his master. The great mark of the Kánphátás is the peculiar splitting of the ear. This is done with a very sharp double edged knife, and is about ¾ of an inch to an inch in length. The ceremony is done in this way. The regular ear-splitter of the sect inserts the knife and asks the novice whether he be willing to renounce the world or not, and that if unwilling, he will withdraw the knife. If the novice says that he is willing to follow the precepts of the sect and become an ascetic, the ear-splitter moves the knife up and down and finishes the operation. A piece of limb tree wood soaked in oil is then put in the wound for three days, and then the ear is washed and the Mûdrá or peculiar earring of the sect is assumed. The Mûdrá is made of only gold, rhinoceros horn, glass or burnt clay, and this earring must always be worn. All Kánphátás also wear a small wooden whistle round their necks, and they sound this at their morning and evening devotions. Kánphátás are forbidden to marry or have intercourse with women. When Kánphátás meet, they salute by using the word Ádesh. The addressed person replies Ádesh. There is an inferior class of ascetics of this sect who are called aghad. They do not split their ears, but are not entitled to equal privileges with the Kánphátá Jogis who have their ears split.

Júnágadh.

Júnágadh, the capital, is in 70° 13' east longitude and 21° 1' north latitude, and situated, as it is, under the Girnár and Dátár hills, is one of the most picturesque towns in India, while in antiquity and historical interest it yields to none. The town is called Karnakûbja in the Girnár Máhátmya, but another Śloka assigns it the following four names in different ages:—

Śloka.

आदौ माणिपुरं नाम चंद्रकेतुपुरं स्मृतं ॥
तृतीयं रैवतं नाम कलौ पौरातनं पुरं ॥

First it was named Manipúr.
In the Smritis it is called Chandraketúpúr.
Thirdly was it named Raivata.
And in this iron age Paurátanpûr.

No reasons are given for the name Manipúr, but Chandraketú appears to have been a Súryavamsi king who worshipped both Shiva and Náráyana with great assiduity, and visited Kailása and Vaikúnth for this purpose. The gods, pleased at his devotion, told him to reside near Mount Raivata, and he accordingly repaired thither and built a city on the old site of Manipúra, which he named after himself Chandraketúpúr. Shiva and Náráyana took up their residence in the vicinity—Shiva at the temple of Bhavnāth, and Náráyana as Dámodar Rái near the Dámodar Kûnd. But both in the Máhátmya and elsewhere, Júnágadh is called simply Dûrg, the Fort. To this day an inhabitant of Sorath will simply call it Gadh (the Fort). Thus an inhabitant of (say) Wanthali or Majevaḍi would, in familiar converse, simply say, "I am going to Gadh to-morrow," and not use the word Júnágadh at all. Júnágadh appears in old writings, &c., as Jirandúrg and Jirangadh, and lastly as Júnágadh. In the old rock inscriptions the city is called Girinagar, Nagar, and in one place Púrwanagar. In the Wanthali inscription it is called Jiran Prákár.

Professor Lassen, in the Indische Alterthumskunde, declares the ancient name to have been Yavanagadh, or fortress of the Yavanas, now corrupted to Júnágadh. And if indeed it were formerly the seat of Persian or Bactrian Satraps, or of the Sah dynasty, such a conjecture seems not unreasonable, and certainly is plausible enough, but I incline to think that the general consensus of the names, Paurátanapúr, Púrwanagar, Jirandúrg,

Jirangadh, and Júnágadh points strongly in the direction that "the ancient fortress" is the real signification of the name.

The Úparkot or citadel is the old or ancient fortress whence Júnágadh probably derives its name, though possibly it may be from the fort on Mount Girnár; both have great claims to antiquity. The ancient archway at the entrance to the Úparkot, within the outer gate, is a fine specimen of the old Hindu Toran or compromise for an arch. The Úparkot also contains most interesting Buddhist caves, and the whole of the ditch and neighbourhood is honey-combed with caves or their remains. The most interesting of these are those called Kháprá Koḍiá near the Telegraph office. These caves have all the appearance of having been once a monastery, and bear the cognizance of the then ruling race, a winged Lion or Griffin. They appear to have been two or three storeys in height. But the quarrymen have been allowed to encroach and injure them, and the lower ones have never been systematically cleared out. Were this done possibly some interesting remains might be discovered.

The caves within the Úparkot evidently formed the residence of a religious establishment, and are fully described by Mr. Burgess in his Antiquities of Kachh and Káthiáwár.

The ditch is cut entirely out of the rock and forms a strong defence. In the Úparkot is the Wáv Aḍi Chaḍi. It is said to have been built by slave girls belonging to the Chúḍásamá rulers of ancient times, one well is called after Rá Noghan. This is very deep and has a wonderful circular staircase inside it. There is also in the Úparkot a mosque built by Súltán Mahmúd Begadhá, but now falling into ruin. Near this mosque there is a large cannon left by the Turks at Diu and brought to Júnágadh by Malik Eiáz, by order of Súltán Bahádúr Sháh. It is called the Lilam Top and is 17 feet long and 7½ feet in circumference at the breech and the diameter of the muzzle is 9½ inches. An inscription on the cannon mentions that the maker of this gun was one Muhammad Hamzah, who lived in the reign of Súltán Sûlimán, son of Salimkhán. Another large cannon called Chûdánál also from Div, is in the southern portion of the fort. It is 13 feet long and has a muzzle 14 inches in diameter. The Úparkot has been many times besieged, and often taken, on which occasions the Rájá was wont to flee to the fort on Mount Girnár, which from its inaccessibility was almost impregnable. The most famous sieges of the Úparkot of which we have any distinct historical account are those by—

Súltán Muhammad Túghlak circa	A. D. 1350
Zúfar Khán (afterwards Súltán Múzafar of Gújarát)	„ 1394
Súltán Áhmad Sháh of Gújarát	„ 1414
Súltán Mahmúd Begadhá of Gújarát..............	„ 1472
Naurang Khán, Syad Kásim, and Gújar Khán...	„ 1591-92

but it was besieged doubtles by the Anhilwárá sovereigns, and probobly by both Múlráj Solankhi and Sidhráj Jayasingh.

There is an inscription of Rá Mandlika, son of Rá Mahipáladeva, within the Úparkot. It is dated Samvat 1507, A.D. 1451.

The fortifications of the town of Júnágadh were all built by the Muhammadans after the capture of the place by Súltán Mahmûd Begadhá of Gújarát, in about A. D. 1472. The town is most picturesque, and the palace is a fine handsome building. Of late years a fine hospital and other public buildings have been erected, and the town has been much improved by fine houses built by the nobles of the Court. Among these the finest is the house of the late minister Jamádár Saleh Hindi, C.I.E. There is also a nice Circle of shops called the Máhábat circle in the front of the palace. There is also a Clock Tower here. The Custom House also is a fine building and so is the residence of Shekh Bahauddin Vazir. A fine guest house has lately been built for Native guests and officials of rank. There are two fine dharamsálás without the Majevdi and Veráwal Gates respectively. The Visalwáo in the town of Júnágadh is said to have been built by Vániá Visal, the traitorous minister of Ráo Mandlik. Ráo

Mandlik is said to have seduced Mohini, the beautiful wife of the minister, who to avenge himself betrayed his master to Súltán Mahmûd. There seems little doubt but that the Úparkot is the ancient Júnágadh, the present town is more correctly called Mustafábád and was built by Mahmûd Begadhá of Gújarát. Below the Úparkot are the caves of Báwá Piárá, a famous Hindu ascetic who is said to have resided in them. But the caves are Buddhist and long anterior to Báwá Piárá whose monastery is not far from these caves and about 100 yards from the Wágeshwari gate. This ascetic gave his name to a well-known ford in the Narmadá river.

Rulers of Júnágadh.

We have no records of any ruling races at Júnágadh previous to the Chúḍásamás except what is contained in the Girnár inscriptions, but it does not seem unlikely that Júnágadh may have been the seat of the ancient Persian satraps, if not of the Sah or Sinha dynasty, who appear to have originally been satraps of Bactria, though afterwards independent. The rule of the Gúptas certainly reached as far as Júnágadh, witness Skandha Gúptas inscription, and it was probably afterwards included in the Valabhi dominions. After this we know, but with no great certainty as to dates, that it passed under the rule of the Chúḍásamás, a Yádav tribe from Thathá in Sindh, and who, originally called Samás, added Chúḍá as a prefix as being descendants of Ráo Chúḍachandra. The history of this tribe is however almost entirely lost, and the bardic legends differ so much as to the names, number, and order of the chieftains, that implicit confidence cannot be placed on them. Nevertheless the accompanying list is no doubt fairly reliable.

I. Chúḍachandra, A.D. 875-907.

The Bardic accounts are unanimous in ascribing the origin of the Chúḍásamás to Chúḍachandra Yádav, a Rájpút of the Samá tribe of Yádavs then ruling at Saminagar, the modern Nagar Thathá in Sindh; and they also agree that before his arrival in the peninsula, Wálá Rám was the Rájá of Wámansthali the modern Wanthali. Some say that Wálá Rám had no son, but that his sister had married the father of Ráo Chúḍachandra of Saminagar, and that the Rájá kept his nephew Ráo Chúḍachandra at Wámansthali, and finally appointed him his successor. Others say that Wálá Rám had a son, but that he quarrelled with Chúḍachandra, and that rather than Chúḍachandra should leave Wámansthali, Wálá Rám expelled his own son. All agree that Chúḍachandra succeeded him. There are very few bardic verses regarding Chúḍachandra, but he is mentioned in the Dhandhusar inscription, and there is a play on his name, viz., that as Chandra Chúḍa (Shiva) placed the moon (chandra) on his head (chuḍá) so Chúḍachandra was considered by the kings of the neighbouring countries as Chúḍásamán or as their head. Hence Chúḍásamá. But no doubt the real derivation is Chúḍá from Chúḍachandra's name, and Samá from the name of his tribe. Possibly, however, the Chúḍásamás may be the ancient Chorasmii or Chorasmians. Chúḍachandra is called Rái Chúḍa in bardic poetry. The Śloka from the Dhandhúsar inscription is as follows :—

आर्या.

श्रीचंद्रचूडचूडाचंद्रं चूडासमानमधृत यतः ॥
जयति नृपहंसवंशोत्तंसः संसत्प्रशंसितो वंशः ॥

Translation.

As Shri Chandrachúḍa (Shiva) places the moon on his head,
So Rájás of the best blood have considered Chúḍachandra as their head.
May this race of his distinguished in all courts, be victorious.

It may I think be considered as beyond a doubt, that Chúḍachandra reigned at Wanthali, and that he founded the rule of the Chúḍásamá tribe in Sorath at the close of the ninth or commencement of the tenth century A. D. or possibly a few years previously. Chúḍachandra had a son named Hamir, but it is doubtful whether he succeeded his father, and it seems most probable that he died during his father's lifetime, and that

Chúḍachandra was succeeded by his grandson Múlráj, the son of Hamir.

Múlráj succeeded his grandfather in A. D. 907, and devoted much attention to foreign wars. He is said to have captured three Rájás of the the north, south, and east respectively, he himself being the Rájá of the west. The Rájá of the south is mentioned in the bardic verse commemorating the achievement as being the Rájá of Asir. Another Rájá is called the Rájá of Gajan, this may be for Gajni in Afghánistán or Gájná, an ancient name of Cambay; the third Rájá is called Som or Somo, but his kingdom is not mentioned. In this poetry Múlráj is described as the son of Hamir. His capital was at Wanthali, though in other bardic poetry he is called lord of Girnár. He was succeeded by his son Vishwavaráh.

II.—Múlráj, A.D. 907 to 915.

Vishwavaráh (the Boar of the world) was a renowned warrior, and famous also for his munificence. He is said to have conquered many lands and bestowed them on poets and others. His fame is said to have reached Mándugadh (Málwá), Párkargadh (Sindh frontier), and Kech Makrán, the Konkan, Kachh, and Kánoj. The bardic poetry commemorating this, calls him son of Múlráj and grandson of Hamir. He was succeeded by his famous son Rá Gáhario or Graharisingh.

III.—Vishwavaráh, A.D. 915-940.

Rá Gáhario succeeded his father in A.D. 940. His name and date make his resemblance to Grah Ripu of the Dwyáshray and Rás Málá, &c., so striking, that there seems little reason to doubt that Grah Ripu was Rá Grahari, which is equivalent to Grah Ripu, *ari* being enemy in Sanscrit. The bardic poetry calls him son of Viswavaráh, and even the kings of Delhi, Devgadh, and Lanká (Ceylon) are represented as trembling at his name. So great was the extent of his rule that it is said that when the ryots brought the State share of their grain (rájbhág) from his most distant frontiers to Júnágadh, most of it used to be consumed by them as food by the way. He was a great friend and ally of Lákhá Phuláni, Rájá of Kachh,

IV.—Gáhario 1st Graharisingh (Grah Ripu), A.D. 940-982.

and was finally defeated by Múlráj of Anhilwáḍá and taken prisoner, but on giving security not to molest the pilgrims to Somnáth was released by him. Lákhá Phuláni was slain in the battle. According to the Dwyáshray (*Indian Antiquary*, page 74, vol. IV.) this Chief built the Úparkot.

V.—Kawát I., A.D. 982-1003.

Rá Kawát succeeded him in A. D. 982 and is said to have fought with Áno, the Lord of Ábu, and to have captured him ten times and ten times released him. This feat is commemorated in the following couplet in which Kawát is described as the son of Gráhario:—

दुहो.

आबुसुत आणो, ग्रह्योग्रहारिउते.
जेणेदशवेळादेवणु, मूक्योअवळीमाण.

There is a well-known legend in Sorath about Rá Kawát. It is said that a Rájá named Viramdeva Parmár* ruled in the Shiál Island, and contrived to capture many Rájás by his stratagems, and confined them there in a wooden cage. At last he captured Rájás of all the 36 races except the Yádav. As he wished to capture Rá Kawát, he persuaded him to visit him on board of his ship which was riding at anchor near Pátan Somnáth, and there treacherously captured him, and sailing off with him to the Shiál Bet confined him there with the other Rájás in the wooden cage. Rá Kawát's maternal uncle was the famous Úgá Wálá of Talájá. On one occasion when all the warriors were relating their achievements before Rá Kawát, all extolled Úgá Wálá so much that the Rá grew jealous, and said to Úgá Wálá that he was a good warrior when aided by Wanthali, but otherwise not of much account. Wálá Úgá, however, boasted that he could manage without the aid of Wanthali, and said metaphorically, that he could clap hands with one palm, *i. e.* without the assistance of the Ráo. He then left the darbár in anger and returned to Talájá. The Rá now in prison

* This Rájá is also called in some versions of the legend Meghánand Chávado.

sent the following message to Wálá Úgá by means of a wandering minstrel (a bard) who had passed by his prison :—

दुहा.

छाती उपर शेरडेा, माया उपर वाढ.
भणजेा वाला उगला, कटपांजरे कवाट.
तुं केतो तक आव्य, ताळी तळाजाधणी.
वाळा हवे वजाड्य, एके हाथे उगला.

Grief at his heart and a wound on his head.
" Say to Úgá Wálá, Kawát is in the wooden cage."
You said that when occasion arose that you Úgá the Wálá lord of Talájá could clap hands with one palm.

On hearing of the capture of Rá Kawát, Wálá Úgá set off with a large army to release him and arrived at the Shiál Bet. After obtaining access to the island by a stratagem, he put the garrison to the sword and slew Viramdeva. In his anxiety to release Kawát he burst open the cage with a kick. In doing this his foot accidentally struck Rá Kawát. Kawát was much enraged at this, and though Úgá Wálá made much submission to him, he treasured up the grudge, and after returning to Wanthali he led an army against Wálá Úgá, and finally killed him near Chitrásar in Bábriáwár, where his páliyo now stands. It is said that Úgá Wálá's sister came to visit her brother's páliyo but found several memorial stones, and knew not which was that of her brother. In her grief, she implored her brother to give her a sign as to which was his páliyo, and on this Úgá Wálá's memorial stone bent forward to greet her. Hence this páliyo does not exactly face the east. It is still bending forward as it is supposed to have done to greet his sister. Kawát was succeeded by his son Dyás.

VI.—Dyás I., also called Mahipál I.—A. D. 1003-1010 ; A. D. 1010-1020 rule of the Pátan Thánahdár.

Rá Dyás succeeded his father in A. D. 1003. During his reign the Rájá of Pátan invaded his dominions and conquered the town of Wanthali. Rá Dyás fled to the Úparkot, to which the Rájá laid siege. Different reasons are assigned for the war, but the accounts are unanimous in representing Rá Dyás to have insulted one of the ladies of the Rájá's family, while on a pilgrimage to Girnar. After much difficulty the Úparkot was taken by a stratagem, soldiers being concealed in covered chariots under the pretence that there were ladies in them. On obtaining entrance to the fort, they massacred the garrison and Rá Dyás was slain. The bards represent Rá Dyás to have given his head in charity to a Cháran, but this is manifestly a legend invented to conceal his defeat. (See *Indian Antiquary* for November 1873.) Ranchodji in his Tárikh-i-Sorath makes out that Júnágadh was taken by Sidhráj Jayasingh of Anhilwárá Pátan, but Sidhráj did not ascend the throne until A. D. 1093-94. After the death of Rá Dyás, his widow, Sorath Ráni, became a Sati, and the Pátan Rájá placed a thánah in Júnágadh and Wanthali. In some bardic poetry Rá Dyás is represented to have captured the Ráná of Chitor, and brought him to Júnágadh as a prisoner, but this is probably bardic exaggeration. When Júnágadh was taken, one of his Ránis fled with his young son Noghan to Eiáwej in Únd, and thence took shelter with Áhir Deváiyat of Álidar Bodidhar. This man is celebrated in local poetry as having allowed his son Wásan to be taken and put to death by the thánahdár in order to save Rá Noghan. It is said that the thánahdár was informed that Rá Dyás's son Noghan was concealed in Deváiyat's house, he therefore sent for him on pretence of inquiring into some village accounts, and then asked him whether Noghan was not concealed in his house. Deváiyat admitted that it was the case, and agreed to send for him. He accordingly wrote a letter to his wife desiring her to send Noghan, but gave the messenger private instructions to send his own son Wásan in his place. Now Noghan was concealed at Álidhar-Bodidhar in Deváiyat's house, and lived there with Deváiyat's son Wásan and his daughter Jásal. When Deváiyat's letter arrived the household were thrown into the greatest grief, for Wásan had only recently been married. Nevertheless though knowing the fate which would await him, Wásan put on his wedding garments and repaired to Júnágadh. When Wásan reached Júnágadh, the thánahdar asked Deváiyat if this were indeed Rá Noghan, and on his replying that it was, he ordered him to slay him, which Deváiyat did without showing any compunction, but uttered under his breath this couplet—

"The mind felt compunction, but this compunction availed nothing.
And he was slain by his own father
In the bazaar of Júnágadh."

It is said that when Wásan was near Júnágadh, he asked the way to the Governor's audience hall. A man pointed it out and asked him to whose wedding he was going, as he was so gaily dressed. "You will see," said Wásan, "if you will accompany me to the Governor's palace." Deváiyat now returned home and devoted all his thoughts to vengeance; he at last engaged all the Áhirs to assemble on the occasion of Jásal's marriage, and promised to deliver the thánahdár into their hands if they would afterwards place Noghan on the throne. They agreed, and Deváiyat repaired to Júnágadh to celebrate the marriage, and requested the thánahdar and his men to honour the marriage with their presence. On their starting for Júnágadh, Jásal spoke as follows to Rá Noghan:—

My mother was weeping near the house,
My sister wept without.
Deváiyat slew Wásan,
That your ancient rule should not pass away from you.

Deváiyat instructed the Áhirs to fall on the thánahdár and his men as soon as the great drum should beat. He took Noghan then with him to the thánahdár's Kacheri, and told him to ask whose drum that was. Noghan did so, and Deváiyat replied—"It is the thánahdár's drum, but you must not beat it else the ráj will be changed." On this Noghan advanced fearlessly, and commenced to beat the drum, and the Áhirs surrounded the thánahdár and his men on all sides and cut down every one of them. They then seated Rá Noghan on the throne. Jásal was afterwards married with great pomp, and Rá Noghan be-

VII.—Rá Noghan I., A. D. 1020-1044.

stowed two villages on her husband with whom she then went to Sindh.

While there, Hamir Sûmro saw and fell in love with her and endeavoured to seize her, but the Áhirs fled, Hamir Sûmro pursued them and she sought aid from Rá Noghan, and sent him some verses reminding him that her brother Wásan's life had been given for him. Rá Noghan now marched on Sindh, and defeated Hamir Sûmro and rescued Jásal. He returned to Sorath and went to Dhári, at which place he is said to have dropped a most valuable ring in the Galdharo Taláv. In order to recover it he tried, but unsuccessfully, to empty the tank. A local couplet records this attempt thus :—

"999 Páwars Noghan employed. Nevertheless the bottom was not reached, and the Galdharo was not a whit dismayed."

VIII.—Rá Khengár I., A. D. 1044-1067.

The author of the Tárikh-i-Sorath says that the army of Rá Noghan was composed of Rájpúts, Áhirs, Káthis, Kolis and Khánts. Rá Khengár succeeded his father, and died after a peaceful reign of 23 years; he was succeeded by his son Noghan.

IX.—Rá Noghan II., A. D. 1067-1098.

This Noghan did not confine his wars to the Peninsula, but offended the great Sidhráj of Anhilwádá, who (Rás Málá, page 119, new edition) compelled him on one occasion to take grass in his mouth and make submission. He also incensed against himself Harráj of Úmetá on the Mahi, and contrived also to have a feud with the Wághelá of Bhoirá in the peninsula. Also he was much displeased with Cháran Mesan, who had insulted him, and he vowed that he would split his (the Cháran's) cheeks.

Rá Noghan had four sons—(1) Bhim, the founder of the houses of Bhadli, Sarwá (whence the Sarvaiyás), and Gámph; (2) Satarsál, who received Dhandhûká; (3) Devghanji, who received the Osham Chorási; and (4) Rá Khengár, who succeeded him. It is said that when Rá Noghan lay a dying, his spirit would not pass from his frame until his sons would promise to perform four behests with which he charged them. These were —(1) to slay Harráj of Úmetá ; (2) to destroy the fort of Bhoirá (now under Jasdan) ; (3) to break down the gate of Pátan ; and (4) to split the cheeks of a Cháran named Mesan who had spoken disrespectfully of him. Khengár alone undertook to perform these four tasks (Rás Málá, new edition, page 119), and poured water into his father's hand as a token that he had sworn to perform these deeds. Then the soul of Noghan was released. As Noghan was proclaimed at Júnágadh, he made that place his capital, though often residing at Wanthali.

X.—Rá Khengár II., A. D. 1098-1125.

Rá Khengár immediately on succeeding to the throne, hearing that Sidhráj was absent warring in Málwá, marched to Pátan, and broke down one of the gates. He carried off the wooden gates to Júnágadh and put them up in the Kálwá (now called Verávwal) gateway at that town. He then advanced to Úmetá, killed Harráj, and washed his blade in the Mahi, and on his return he passed by Bhoirá and broke down the fortress thereof. When he returned to Júnágadh he sent for the Cháran and filled his mouth with gold, until he said "my cheeks are split ;" afterwards he bestowed on him the village called after him Mesanká. It is about 12 miles to the south-west of Pálitáná. Rá Khengár married the celebrated Ránik Devḍi, who had been sought in marriage by Sidhráj Jayasingh, and this fresh injury eventually caused that monarch to march against the Rá. He laid siege to Júnágadh and finally took the Úparkot. It is said that Rá Khengár used to stay himself at the Úparkot, but kept Ránik Devḍi in his palace in the fortress of Girnár. His nephews, Visal and Desal, were the only persons allowed access there except the guard. Rá Khengár used to go from the Úparkot to the Girnár fortress to visit Ránik Devḍi, and one day found Desal there drunk, and in spite of all his protestations, accused him of an improper intimacy with her. Finally he expelled both Desal and Visal, who at once went to Sidhráj, and by obtaining entrance to the Úparkot with some cattle carrying grain, they slew the guards and attacked the palace. The Rá came forth and fought and fell in the battle, and the Úparkot was taken. After this Desal and Visal took Sidhráj up to the Girnár fortress, and asked their aunt to open the gate. She did so, not knowing what had happened. Then Sidhraj entered, and on seeing her two sons, ordered them to be put to death. He now took Ránik Devḍi with him, and returned towards Pátan. At Wadhwán, overcome by the noble bearing of Ránik Devḍi, he offered to make her his first queen, but she told him that nothing would make her forgive him the death of her innocent boys. Then '*Sat*' coming on her, she cursed Sidhráj, and warned him that he should die sonless. After this she mounted the funeral pile and was burned with her husband's turban on her lap. Ránik Devḍi's memorial-stone stands in Wadhwán to this day. Her curse was fulfilled, and Sidhráj died childless. Some of the verses of this ballad of Rá Khengár and Ránik Devḍi are very poetical. Many are given in the Rás Málá, but not, I think, the following :—

> For shame, murderous Girnár,
> Why were you not bent crooked
> When died Rá Khengár?
> Thus wept Ranik Devḍi.

XI.—Rá Noghan III., A. D. 1125-1140.

Shortly after Sidhráj's return, the inhabitants of Júnágadh rose and expelled his thánahdár and seated Noghan III. on the throne. This chieftain does not make a figure in history, and probably was careful not to attract the notice of the sovereigns of Pátan. He died in 1140 A.D. and was succeeded by his son Kawát, who ruled in an equally unobtrusive manner, and after a short reign of 12 years was succeeded by his son called Jayasingh called also Gário and Dyás.

XII.—Rá Kawát II., A. D. 1140-1152.

XIII.—Rá Gário II. called also Jayasingh and Dyás, A. D. 1152-1169.

The bards explain that the names Dyás and Gário are both titles, Dyás meaning the giver and Gário (Gráhario) the seizer. They say that the real name of this chieftain was Jayasingh, but that his seizing on Kánoj obtained for him the title of Gário, and his munificence caused him to be known as Dyás. His seizure of Kánoj is thus explained. Jayasingh was a connection of the celebrated Jayachandra of Kánoj, and is said to have been left by that chieftain in charge of Kánoj when Jayachandra went forth to war with Prathiráj Chohán. On Jayachandra's return defeated, Jayasingh refused to permit him to enter, and retained possession of the place. For this achievement he was called Rá Gráhario or Gário. Subsequently terms were arranged between Jayachandra and Jayasingh, and the latter returned to Sorath conquering Gwálior on his return journey, and defeating the Rájá of Mewár. Jayasingh afterwards joined the sovereign of Gújarát, Bhimdeva, in his warfare with Prathiráj, and is alluded to in the Prathiráj Rásá as Chúdásamá Jayasingh (Rás Mála, page 166, new edition). On the death of this chieftain, his Ráni burned herself with him on his funeral pile. He was succeeded by his son Ráisingh.

XIV.—Rá Ráisingh, A.D. 1180-1184.

Ráisingh reigned four years, and was succeeded by his son Mahipál 2nd. Ráisingh is said to have fought with the celebrated Prathiráj Chohán.

XV.—Rá Mahipál II., A.D. 1184-1201, also called Gajráj.

This chieftain was also called Gajráj. The Rájá Wachráj of Sirsá (North-West Provinces) invaded Sorath in the reign of Gajráj and marched against Júnágadh, but was defeated and taken prisoner by Gajráj. Afterwards Gajráj sent his senápati Chúḍámani and an army to Hindûsthán, and declared that he would give his daughter Motináde to whomsoever should be able to defeat him. Chûḍámani marched to Máhobá, where resided Ålá and Údal, maternal cousins of Mal Khán, son of Wachráj, Rájá of Sirsá, who had succeeded his father on the gádi. They accepted Chûḍámani's challenge on behalf of Mal Khán and defeated his army, Údal vanquishing Chúḍámani in single combat. Then the marriage was agreed upon, but it was arranged that another battle should take place at Júnágadh, and each party invited their supporters to fight. On Mal Khán's side was

Lákhan of Kánoj, Rámayá of Gújargadh, Rájá Prathipat, Rájá Makrandá of Mohangadh, and others; while on Gajráj's side were many chieftains of equal rank. After some fighting Gajráj was worsted and Mal Khán was married to Motináde. Mahipál was succeeded by his son Jayamal. Rá Jayamal's praises are celebrated in the Jayamal Jaswarnan. He is said to have been both brave, handsome, and accomplished. He was succeeded by his son Mehepo. The following duho is said of Rá Jayamal:—

XVI.—Rá Jayamal, A.D. 1201-1230.

The Dámodar Kúnd, Kúnwar Mehepo,
And the old fortress and Mount Girnár,
Such things belong to no other house,
But all four belong to the house of Chûḍ.*

Many Rájás are said to have presented Jayamal with horses as tribute.

Rá Mehepo succeeded his father in A. D. 1230. In his reign the Káthis became very headstrong and rebelled, and assembled their forces at Kotrá. They defeated the Rá's minister Motichand, who marched against them. The Wáḷá Chief of Dhánk alone supported the Rá, who now marched against the Káthis with a powerful army and drove them from their villages. On the Rá's return to Júnágadh, however, the Káthis returned. The Káthis during this warfare seized several villages belonging to Dhánk. He was succeeded by his son Khengár.

XVII.—Rá Mehepo, A. D. 1230-1253, also called Mahipál III.

Rá Khengár succeeded his father in A. D. 1253. He followed up his father's successes against the Káthis and expelled them from the Dhánk villages which they had occupied, and restored them to the Dhánk chieftain, and compelled the Káthis to agree to service. The chief men at Rá Khengár's court were Wálá Arjanji of Dhánk, a Wálá Rájpút, and Kalián Seth. These two disagreeing, the post of chief minister was given to

XVIII.—Rá Khengár III., A. D. 1253-1260.

* Chúd short for Chúdachandra.

Málan Mehtá. Kalián Seth indignant at his supersession caused Málan Mehtá to be assassinated. This came to the Rá's ears and he put Kalián Seth to death and appointed Málan Mehtá's son, Mahidhar, as chief minister. When Kalián Seth's son Lowo grew up he fled to Delhi, and finally at the close of the next reign persuaded the emperor to send an army to Gújarát. Rá Khengár and Arjanji are said to have ravished a Mer female. Her cries attracted her kindred who wounded both Arjanji and the Rá so grievously that they subsequently both died of their wounds.

XIX.—Rá Mandlik I., A. D. 1260-1306.

During Rá Mandlik's time Álagh Khán conquered Gújarát on the part of Sûltán Alá-ûd-din Khiljy; he also destroyed Somnáth, which had been rebuilt since the time of Mahmûd Ghaznavi, and conquered the sea coast of the peninsula from Goghá to Mádhavapûr. On this occasion Rá Mandlik is said to have defeated a division of his troops, but possibly he may have defeated one of the Muhammadan governors of the sea coast left by Álagh Khán. Whichever may be the exact truth, he is styled in the Revati Kûnda inscription as conqueror of the Moghals. In the Girnár inscription he is mentioned as having adorned the temple of Neminàth with gold plates. We learn from the Wanthali inscription that a (Ráthor) chieftain named Jagatsing wrested Wanthali from him (in about A. D. 1261) and this family ruled there under five successive chiefs for four distinct generations. It seems possible that these Ráthoḍs were the ancestors of the Wájás of Somnáth, and their alliance with the Wághelás of Dholká would explain their ability to hold so important a town as Wanthaḷi without molestation. Rá Mandlik was succeeded by Noghan IV.

XX.—Rá Noghan IV., A. D. 1306-1308.

Rá Noghan IV. was of middle age when he succeeded to the gádi. He is praised in the Girnár inscription as a mighty warrior. He reigned only for two years and was succeeded by his son Mahipál IV. This inscription calls the Chûḍásamás of the Yáḍav stock.

XXI.—Rá Mahipál IV., A. D. 1308-1325.

Rá Mahipál succeeded his father and repaired the temple of Somnáth, and gave much money for religious uses. After a reign of 17 years he was succeeded by his son Khengár.

XXII.—Rá Khengár IV., A. D. 1325-1351.

Rá Khengár succeeded his father in 1325. He expelled the Muhammadan governors from Somnáth and restored the ancient glory of the temple. But in his reign Sûltán Muhammad Tûghlak invaded Gújarát, and besieged and took Júnágadh, and took Rá Khengár prisoner and subdued the country. In this battle Wághelá Vir, a devoted adherent of Khengár, was slain. Rá Khengár was however soon released; he now turned his attention to putting down piracy and acquiring a footing on the sea shore, and is said to have conquered the eighteen islands on the coast. Rá Khengár was a great patron of music. He is said in the Mandlik Kávya to have subdued 84 minor chieftains, Jhálás and Gohils included. He was succeeded by his son Jayasingh.

XXIII.—Rá Jayasingh, A. D. 1351-1369.

Rá Jayasingh succeeded his father in 1351. He is said in the Mandlik Kávya to have been victorious over his enemies. The Muhammadan rulers of the sea coast and Somnáth country, who had been re-apppointed by Muhammad Tûghlak, appear to have retained their posts. In his time the emperor Firoz Tûghlak came to Gújarát. Rá Jayasingh was succeeded by his son Mahipál.

XXIV.—Rá Mahipál V., also called Mahipati, A. D. 1369-1373.

Rá Mahipál V. succeeded his father and recovered Wanthali from Amarsingh and Tejsingh, the descendants of Jagatsingh; he was succeeded by his brother Mûktasingh or Mokalsingh.

XXV.—Rá Mûktasingh, A. D. 1373-1397.

Rá Mûktasingh succeeded his brother, and reigned for 24 years, during which time he appears to have devoted himself to promoting literature and preserving peace with his neighbours. He was succeeded by his son Mandlik 2nd. Zûfar Khán, afterwards Sûltán Mûzafar, exacted tribute from him, after his expedition in 1394, and previously to this he, agreeably to the orders of the Viceroy of Gûjarát on behalf of Sûltán Firoz Tûghlak, who placed a thánahdár at Jûnágadh, removed his capital from Júnágadh to Wanthali and obeyed this sovereign's orders. By this monarch's order he marched against Ghûmli, and subdued the chieftains of the coast. This appears from the Dhandhûsar inscription. His minister's name was Gadádhar, and after him his son Vijayanáth who built the wáv at Dhandhúsar in which this inscription is found in St. 1445, A. D. 1389. He was succeeded by his son Mandlik.

XXVI.—Rá Mandlik II., A. D. 1397-1400.

Rá Mandlik succeeded his father in A. D. 1397, but does not appear to have made a very prominent figure in the history of the time; he remained at Wanthali, and died in 1400, and was succeeded by his brother Melak or Melag.

XXVII.—Rá Melak or Melag or Meligdev, A. D. 1400-1415.

Rá Melak succeeded his brother in A. D. 1400. He expelled the thánahdár from Júnágadh and again made that city his capital. He appears from the Mandlik Kávya* to have sheltered a Jhálá chieftain fleeing from Sûltán Áhmad (probably Satarsál). In A. D. 1413-14 Sûltán Áhmad marched against Júnágadh.† On this occasion Rá Meligdev fought a pitched battle with Sûltán Áhmad at Wanthali, but was defeated, and fled to Júnágadh.‡ Wanthali was taken by Sûltan Áhmad, who then marched to Jûnágadh and took the lower fortress (the Úparkot), but the Rájá escaped by fleeing to the upper fortress of Girnár. But the Mirat-i-Sikandri adds—"The greater part of the zamindárs of Sorath became submissive and obedient, and consented to service." And it further appears that he left two officers to collect the zamindár's tribute (salámi). The Mandlik Kávya, however, omits all account of the fight at Wanthali and represents that Rá Melak defeated Áhmad Sháh and plundered his baggage, but this is probably an exaggeration based on the Rá's escape to the Girnár

* See Dhrángadhra History, Gújarát History, and Mirat-i-Sikandri.
† Mirat-i-Sikandri.
‡ Mirat-i-Sikandri and Memorial-stones at Wanthali.

fortress and his avoidance of capture. In the Úparkot inscription Melakdev is styled the Yádav Ráná of Jirandúrg. He was succeeded by his son Jayasingh.

XXVIII.—Rá Jayasingh III., A.D. 1415-1440.

Rá Jayasingh succeeded his father in A. D. 1415. During his reign, Sûltán Áhmad was too much occupied by Gûjarát and Málwá affairs to again visit Sorath. The Revati Kúnd inscription says that he defeated the Yavan in the battle at the fort of Jhánjharkot. It is difficult to identify this place, but it was probably Jhánjhmer, which, as named after Wálá Jhánjharsi, might well be called Jhánjharkot. He was succeeded in A. D. 1440 by his brother Mahipal IV.

XXIX.—Rá Mahipál IV., A. D. 1440-1451.

Rá Mahipál succeeded his brother in A. D. 1440. He was most devoted to religion and entertained all the Dwárká and Somnáth pilgrims at his own charges. He was also a devoted worshipper of Dámodar Rái (a name of Krishná) and practised much ascetism in order to procure a son. A son was born to him eventually and named Mandlika.

XXX.—Rá Mandlika, III., A.D. 1451-1472.

Rá Mandlika succeeded his father in A. D. 1451. He was educated by his father with great care, and was skilled in all sciences, but specially in the use of arms. When he was of a fitting age, he was married to Kûntádevi, the daughter of Arjûn, son of Bhim Gohil. Arjûn had fallen fighting with the Mûsalmáns, and his daughter had been brought up in Dûdá Gohil's house. Dûdá was brother of Arjûn and was chieftain of Arthilá. During Mahipál's life he installed Mandlika on the throne and all the neighbouring Rájás offered presents except Sángan Wádhel of Bet. Mandlika accordingly marched against him and defeated him and took him prisoner, after vanquishing him in single combat. Then after taking from him much plunder, he released him, and returned victoriously to Júnágadh. The Mirat-i-Sikandri speaks of Bhim, the son of Ságar, which is probably a slip of the pen for Sángan. At this time the Sûltán of Áhmadábád sent him a message complaining that Dûdá Gohil was ravaging his territory, and requesting Rá Mandlika to restrain him. The Rá replied that the Sûltán's enemies were his enemies and at once marched against him. Dûdo putting on his armour marched to oppose him ; after some fighting between the two armies, Dûdo came up to Mandlika and said to him, that he must not consider him like Sángan Wádhel, that he (Mandlika) was but a youth and was besides the husband of his niece and might have a son by her, and hence that it would be early for him to die now, he therefore counselled him to withdraw from the battle. Mandlika however replied that he was the son of a Kshatri and therefore could not retreat. The warriors then engaged. Dûdo begged Mandlika to strike first, but Mandlika replied—"If you do not strike first, you will never again get a chance." On this Dûdo made a blow at Mandlika which he warded, and dealt Dûdo such a blow that his head fell from his body. Dûdo's army was now put to the rout and Mandlika returned and made a triumphal entry into Júnágadh after sacking and destroying Arthilá.* He now desired to marry another wife, and after consulting his ministers made proposals for the hand of Úmábái, daughter of Bhimsinghji of Kûwá, who was then (as his father Wanvirji was ruling at Kûwá) residing at Sithá. Her father agreed, and finally Rá Mandlika went to Sithá and married her with great pomp. He was not however blessed with a son by her and therefore married many other Chandravamsi Jhálás and Suryavamsi† Gohils, but still remained sonless. However, eventually he had sons. Sángan Wádhel now again rebelled and Rá Mandlika marched against him and occupied Bet, Sángan Wádhel fleeing with his family. He, however, obtained foreign aid, and again opposed Mandlika as he was returning, but Mandlika routed him and again took him prisoner, but however again released him. In his reign flourished the celebrated Narsi Mehta, a devotee of Vishnû, very famous in the province. It is said that Vinjal Wájo, chief of Pátan Somnáth, was a great friend of Rá Mandlika. Vinjal was attacked by leprosy and consequently

* Arthilá is still waste; after the sack of Arthilá, this branch of the Gohils moved their capital to Láthi.

† Thus says the Mandlika Kávya.

resolved to make a pilgrimage to Banáras, and failing to be cured there to perish in the snows of Kailás. The Bráhmans, however, told him that before doing this he must first make a pilgrimage to Girnár. Vinjal was anxious to avoid doing this as his friend Mandlika would see him in his diseased state. But as the Bráhmans insisted that it was necessary for him to visit Girnár, he went secretly thither and bathed at the Dámodar Kûnda and bestowed a small gold image of an elephant on the Bráhmans in charity. After his departure a dispute arose between the Bráhmans as to a division of the gold, and the question was referred to the Rá, who at once asked who gave the gold elephant. On hearing that it was Vinjal Wájo, he set out after him. When he reached the stream now called Gangájalio between Wadál and Káthrotá, he there met a man bearing his daily supply of Ganges water which was sent to him each day from Hindûstán. In his anxiety to overtake Vinjal, he bathed with his clothes on, *i.e.* simply poured the Ganges water over himself, clothes and all, and went on to Jetalsar, where he found Vinjal Wájo encamped. Vinjal begged him not to approach him as he had the loathsome disease of leprosy. But Rá Mandlika would not be denied, and advanced and embraced him, and immediately Vinjal's leprosy was cleansed. From this circumstance the stream where Rá Mandlika met the carrier of Ganges water has been ever since called the Gangájalio, and Rá Mandlik also is called by this epithet.

There are two distinct stories told of the causes of the fall of Rá Mandlika, but the most popular is that told by Ranchodji in the Tárikh-i-Sorath, besides being known by every Bard and Cháran within the peninsula. They say that Nágbái was a beautiful Cháráṇ female of the village of Moniá near Sarsái and as chaste as she was beautiful. Rá Mandlika who had heard much of the beauty of her son's wife went to Monia on the pretext of hunting in order to see her, and was so inflamed by her charms, that he placed his hand on her bosom. She turned instantly away from him and Nágbái cursed him saying, "The bride of thy good fortune shall turn away her face from thee even as I do now, and will unite herself with the Muhammadan kings."

So saying she left him, and Rá Mandlika returned discomfited and ashamed to Júnágadh. The following dûho is also said to have been said by Nágbái. It is interesting, both because Júnágadh is styled Gadh, and because the cure of Vinjal Wájo is mentioned:—

दुहो

गंगाजळ गढेशा, पंड ताहारुं हुतुं पवित्र.
वींजाने रगत गयां, मनेतो वाळा मंडलीक.

Oh lord of the Gadh, your body was so pure from Ganges water,
That you cleansed Vinjá of leprosy,
But bestowed on me a guinea-worm, oh Mandlik !

Another story is, that Rá Mandlika seduced Man Mohan, the beautiful wife of his minister Wániá Visal, who in revenge invited Sûltán Mahmûd of Gûjarát to invade Rá Mandlika's dominions, and thus betrayed his master. Anyhow in A.D. 1467 Sûltán Mahmûd attacked Júnágadh, but on receiving the submission of Rá Mandlika returned to his capital. Next year on the pretext that the Rá affected independent rank, &c., he again sent an army against him and again withdrew it on receiving his submission. But in 1469 he resolved to conquer the country and marched thither with a large force. After a long and gallant defence Rá Mandlika surrendered in A.D. 1472-73, and his dominions were annexed to the Gûjarát Saltanat. Rá Mandlika himself was converted to Islám and received the title of Khán Jahán, and lies buried in the Mánik Chok at Áhmadábád. Sûltán Mahmûd changed the name of Júnágadh to Mûstafábád and built the fortifications round the town, and the mosque in the Úparkot. And for a short time he took up his residence there, and caused his nobles also to construct palaces in that town. He sent also for Syads, Kázis, and other Muhammadans, and gave them jágirs and official appointments, and directed them to spread the religion of Islám. From this date to the close of the Gûjarát monarchy, Júnágadh was governed by an official appointed direct from Áhmadábád styled a thánáhdár. This official collected the tribute and revenue of the crown domain, but the Sûltán also placed Rájá Mandlika's son in Júnágadh as a jágirdár. The name of this son was Bhûpatsingh. The first

A.D. 1472 to A.D. 1505.
Bhúpatsingh, jágirdár, otherwise called Melag.

Thánahdárs.
1. Tátár Khán.
2. Mirzá Khalil (afterwards Súltan Múzafar II.)

thánahdár was Tátár Khán, an adopted son of the Sûltán, and after him Mirzá Khalil, the eldest son of the Sûltán, who afterwards succeeded him under the title of Sûltán Mûzafar. Prince Khalil during his tenure of office founded the village called Khalilpûr. The jágir allotted to Bhûpatsingh was the Sil Bagasrá chovisi, and his descendants may be found there to this day, but he resided in Júnágadh. Bhûpatsingh was succeeded by his son Khengár.

A.D. 1503 to A.D. 1525
Jágirdár.
Khengár.
Thánahdárs.
1. Mirzá Khalil.
2. Malik Eiáz.
3. Tátár Khán Ghori.

After the accession of Sûltán Mûzafar and indeed during the latter part of Sûltán Mahmûd's reign, the seat of government was removed from Júnágadh to Div owing to the importance of that island as a naval station, and to check the ravages of the Portuguese. Tátár Khán Ghori was left at Júnágadh by Malik Eiáz, who himself resided at Div. After the disgrace and death of Malik Eiáz, Tátár Khán Ghori became independent at Júnágadh, and after the death of Sûltán Bahadûr the Ghori family reigned independently at Júnágadh, though still owing a nominal allegiance to the successive Sûltáns at Áhmadábád. This state of affairs continued until the first conquest of Gújarát by Akbar, when Áminkhán Ghori had succeeded his father Tátár Khán at Júnágadh.

Jágirdár.
Noghan, A.D. 1525-1551.
Thanahdars.
Malik Eiáz.
Tátár Khán Ghori.

Khengár was succeeded by his son Noghan in A.D. 1525 and he lived until A.D. 1551. Tátár Khán Ghori had now become almost independent. In his time Jám Ráwal conquered Hálár and built Nawánagar. Noghan was succeeded by his son Shrisingh in A. D. 1551.

Jágirdár.
Shrisingh, A.D. 1551-1586.
Muhammadan Rulers.
Tátár Khán Ghori.
Ámin Khán Ghori.

He lived till 1586. During his time Tátár Khán Ghori died and was succeeded by his son Ámin Khán Ghori. In his time too Akbar conquered Gújarát, though Sorath yet remained independent under the Ghori rule. The exact date of Tátár Khán Ghori's death is not known, but from the mention of Ámin Khán as his successor it must have been from about A. D. 1570 to 1575. On the return of the emperor Akbar to Ágrah in A. D. 1573 after the defeat and death of Muhammad Husain Mirzah and Ikhtiyár-ûl-Mûlk he gave orders that Sorath should be conquered from Ámin Khán Ghori. Wazir Khán attempted it but was unequal to the task. Great confusion existed now in Sorath. The Moghal conquest of Gújarát, the collapse of the power of the Gújarát Sûltáns, the encróachments of the Jám, and the assumption of independence by the Ghoris all augmented the confusion, afterwards increased by the escape and partizan warfare of Sûltán Mûzafar in A. D. 1583.

Jágirdár.
Khengár, A.D. 1586-1591. But he retired to Bagasrá as a tálukdár and lived till A. D. 1608.

Muhammadan rulers.
Ámin Khán Ghori.
Daulat Khán Ghori.

During these disturbances, Ámin Khán Ghori and his son Daulat Khán Ghori espoused the cause of Múzafar as did the Jám and Lomá Khûmán of Kherdi. The exact date of Ámin Khán Ghori's death is not known, but it was in about A. D. 1589-90. Ráizádah Khengár also warmly espoused Mûzafar's side. After the siege and capture of Júnágadh in A.D. 1591-92 by Naurang Khán, Syad Kásim, and Gûjar Khán, Khengár was dismissed to his estate of Sil-Bagasrá, and the Ráizádahs (as these later Chûḍásamás were called) ceased to rule at Júnágadh. Daulat Khán Ghori died of his wounds during the siege, and from henceforth Júnágadh became the seat of the imperial foujdárs of Sorath, in subordination to the imperial viceroy at Áhmadábád.

The first foujdár of Júnágadh was Naurang Khán and next Syad Kásim, and the most famous were (1) Mirzah Isá Tarkhán, (2) Kûtb-ûd-din Kheshgi, and (3) Sardárkhán.

Of these Mirzah Isá Tarkhán ruled Sorath from about A. D. 1633-34 to A.D. 1642, when he was appointed viceroy of Gújarát. On this occasion he left his son Ináyat Úllah as foujdár at Júnágadh, and himself repaired to the capital of Gújarát (Áhmadábád) to conduct the government. In Mirzah Isá

Tarkhán's time the fortifications of Júnágadh were entirely repaired.

Kûtb-ûd-din was another famous foujdár, his tenure of office lasted from about 1653-1666. He in about A.D. 1664 conquered Nawánagar, and annexed it to the imperial domain.

Sardárkhán also distinguished himself while foujdár of Sorath both by the firmness of his rule, and by his construction of the Sardár Bágh and excavation of the Sardár Taláo. He built a mausoleum for himself in the Sardár Bágh, but died at Thathá in Sindh and is said to have been buried there and not at Júnágadh. He was foujdár from about 1666 to 1686, but in 1670 he went for a short time to Idar and was replaced by Syad Dilerkhán. The date of the construction of the Sardár Bágh is A. H. 1092, A. D. 1681.

The last of the foujdárs was Sherkhán Bábi, who afterwards became independent and assumed the title of Nawáb Bahádûr Khán.

KESOD.

Kesod, called in the Persian histories Kesoj, is situated on the bank of an affluent of the Sábi river called the Tilori. It is about fifteen miles south of Wantháli and 25 south-west of Júnágadh. It is a thriving town with a population of 3,169 according to the census of 1872, but fell to 2,589 after the famine of 1878-79. The population consists chiefly of Lohánás. Kesod is a walled town with an inner citadel. Kesod was originally a Ráizádah holding, and Dagoji Ráizádah figured prominently in the local wars of the eighteenth century, but in A.D. 1784-86 he became so troublesome by ravaging the parganah of Bántwá, that the tálúkdárs of that estate, Bábis Edal Khán and Mûkhtiyár Khán, sought the aid of the Júnágadh Diwán Raghunáthji, who sent his brothers Dûlabhji and Ranchodji to suppress his outrages. They thoroughly humbled Dagoji and forced him to pay a fine, as well as to restore the plunder of Bántwá. Eventually, being unable to defray the demands of his soldiery, he sold Kesod in A.D. 1788 for a lakh of Jámsháhi koris. The Ráizádahs still hold grás in the Kesod parganah.

KHORÁSÁ.

This village lies about five and a half miles to the south-east of Bhandûri, and twelve miles to the north-west of Pátan Somnáth. In 1872 the population was 778, but increased to 1,066 in 1881, owing to immigration from the neighbouring villages. A very interesting inscription in the temple of the Nágnáth Máhádeva at Chorwár is said to have been brought thither from Khorásá. This inscription, which is dated $\frac{\text{St. 1445}}{\text{A.D. 1389}}$, affords much historical information. It has been erroneously translated by Colonel Tod (Tod's Western India). This inscription makes special mention of repairs made by one Mal to the temple of the Sun at Khorásá. Mal is described to have been a Kshatri of the Rohilá tribe of the Makwáná race, also called Mál or Máldé, and to have been appointed as local Governor of Khorásá by Vanráj Shivráj. This Shivráj is probably the same as Shivgan Wájá of the Phûlká and Bhûa Timbi lekhs. The inscription at Chorwár gives the genealogy of this Mal or Máldé and of his wife Vimladevi. His ancestor Lûning came to Sauráshtrá from Márwár; Luning's son Bhimsingh received in grás the villages of Panchálá, Kálej, &c. Bhimsingh's son Lavanya Pál died at Kálej, leaving 3 sons (1) Lakshma Singh, (2) Lakhan Pál, and (3) Laksh (Lakho?); of these Lakshma Singh was slain in battle at Júnágadh, leaving a son Ráj Singh, who was the father of Máldé; Ráj Singh, who was a brave and gallant man, was killed in battle at Bet Shankhodhár. The wife of Máldé was Vimládevi of the Parmár race. Máldé had three brothers, namely, (1) Matráj (Mátrá), (2) Mûnj (Munjo?), and (3) Mohan, who was slain while endeavouring to recover cows driven from Khorásá by robbers. Matráj married a wife named Námalde, by whom he had four sons: (1) Limbo, (2) Harráj, (3) Wághelá, (4) Mûlráj. Máldé himself had six sons: (1) Dûdo, (2) Lákho, (3) Devo, (4) Rámo, (5) Sángo, (6) Lunsi, and one daughter named Hánsi. Máldé's mother Rantádevi's great-grandfather was Wághela Kshemráj of Karkarpûri in Márwár. His son was Sombhram, his son was Vir (Viro), who came to Sauráshtrá and took service with Rá Khengár IV. of Júnágadh, and took part in the battle between that chief and

Sûltán Muhammad Tûghlak. On this occasion Viro sent away Rá Khengár* on the shoulders of his brother's son Bhimdeva, and himself gave his life in his defence. Rantádevi, mother of Máldé, was daughter of this Viro. The river Kálipát, an affluent of the river Megal, flows to the south of the village. There are two tanks at Khorásá, one of which is called Jámbwálû. There is a Government vernacular school at Khoili

Koili.

This is a village belonging to the Wanthali Mahál of the Júnágadh State, and is about four and a half miles distant from Wanthali to the north-east. It is principally famous for the Tarnetar monastery within its village lands. The population of Koili consisted in 1872 of 1,300 souls, but this number fell to 1,192 in 1881, owing to the ravages of the famine of 1878-79. Koili is said to derive its name from the Koel or Indian cuckoo, which abounds in the groves here. The village was granted in $\frac{\text{Sumwat 1784}}{\text{A.D. 1728}}$ to Máhant Tulsigarji by the then Fáujdár of Júnágadh, and the successive Máhants or abbots have ever since been famous for purity of life, learning and general benevolence. Their hospitality is specially famous, and in times of famine they have frequently supported large numbers of starving folk, so much so that there are several bardic verses in praise of different abbots, and specially of Kripálgar, who dispensed much charity in the famine of $\frac{\text{Samwat 1869}}{\text{A.D. 1813}}$. In $\frac{\text{Samwat 1887}}{\text{A.D. 1831}}$ when Nawáb Báhádûr Khán was on the gádi of Júnágadh, and when Damodargar was abbot of Tarnetar, the Nawáb visited Tarnetar. The abbot received him right royally, and the Nawáb was so pleased that he granted to the monastery the two villages of Bodkû and Rangpûr, and also bestowed on the abbot himself an elephant, a palanquin, and a torch as a personal honour.

The abbots of Tarnetar have always been fond of horse-breeding, and to this day there are a good stock of horses and mares at the monastery.

The name Tarnetar is a corruption of the Sanskrit Trinetra,

* Note.—This probably alludes to Rá Khengár's escape to the fortress of Girnár.

three-eyed, an epithet of Siva, to whom the temple is sacred. This temple was repaired by the Gáekwar's Diván Vithal Ráo Dewáji in $\frac{\text{Samwat 1867}}{\text{A.D. 1811}}$, and there is an inscription to this effect in the temple. But its original foundation is attributed to an ascetic named Bhagwánnáth, who lived solely on milk and came to this spot from Anjár in Kachh in $\frac{\text{Samwat 1321}}{\text{A.D. 1265}}$ during the reign of Rá Noghan of Júnágadh. There is a large fair held here on the 8th of the light half of the month of Ásu, which lasts for two days, and is attended by over 1,000 people. There is an image of Ganesh in the temple enclosure, in the great toe of the right foot of which there grows a small banyan tree, which is said to have always the same number of leaves, namely seven, and to be always of the same size. It is called the Akshaya Wad or "imperishable banyan."

Kútiáná.

Kûtiáná is situated on the bank of the river Bhádar about twenty-five miles east of Porbandar. It is a fortified town, and has an inner citadel, and is the head-quarters of a mahál or revenue division. A Wahiwatdár or Revenue official, and a 1st Class Magistrate reside here. The soil around Kûtiáná is very fertile, and large crops are raised by irrigation. The population by the census of 1872 was 9,912 souls, but this number decreased to 8177 in 1881 consequent on the famine of 1878-79. The name Kûtiáná is said to be derived from a Cháran female named Kûnti, who used to graze her flocks there, and eventually founded a nes or hamlet on the spot where the town now stands. This gradually grew into a village, and was called after Kûnti, Kûntiáná, now corrupted into Kûtiáná. Old Kûtiáná or Sákûkáno timbo is about a mile to the west of the modern town, and there are the remains of the foundations of the fort; it fell waste in about A. D. 1200, and shortly afterwards the present town was founded. There is an old well at old Kûtiáná, which contains the image of a Kshetrapál or local deity, and newly-married couples go there to this day to make offerings and pay their adorations. This spot is said to have been the ancient Kûndinpûr, the residence of King Bhishmak, the father of Rûkmini, the head wife of Krishna. She had heard of the fame of Krishna and wished to marry him, and he also was desirous of marrying her, but her brother Rûkhmi or Rûkhmayo interfered and persuaded Bhishmak to marry her to Shishûpál, the Rájá of Chedidesh. On hearing that this was settled, Rûkmini wrote a letter to Krishna at Dwarká, entreating him to interfere and carry her off, or else she would be married to Shishûpál, and that if he would not rescue her, she would die. She also said in her letter that it was not fit that the jackal should take the prey of the lion, and told him that he would find her at the temple of Ambiká, without the city, the day before her nuptials with Shishûpál. This note she despatched to Dwarká by a trusty Bráhman. Krishna on reading it at once set out and reached Kûndinpûr in one night, and next morning carried off Rûkhmini on the morning of the wedding day. A great battle ensued with Shishûpál and his men, but Krishna was victorious; but Rûkhmayo, the brother of Rûkhamani, who had taken an oath to slay Krishna and rescue his sister and else never to re-enter the town, still pursued him. A battle was fought, but Rûkhmayo was defeated and captured, and released only after his moustaches had been shaven off with swords.

Krishna then carried off Rûkhmini to Madhavpore, and there married her according to the Rákshas Viwá ceremony. Rûkhmayo, unable to re-enter Kûndinpûr, established the village called Bhojkat, about three miles south of Kûtiáná. This village is now known as Kátwáná. Kutiáná has always been famous for its bards and poets, and the following celebrated bards and poets flourished there :—

(1) Bhát Ráo Lakhan.
(2) Sorathiá Sárasvat Vainkunth.
(3) Kshatri Hardás Bhagat.
(4) Bhát Thakûrdás.
(5) Bhát Bhúpatsingh.

Kûtiáná was called Mûzafarábád by the Mûhammadans, because it is said that Sûltan Mûzafar Halim of Gúzarát, who, when yet a prince, was viceroy of Sorath, was very fond of the place, and made it very populous and built the fort. In old Persian deeds,

&c., this town is styled Mûzafarábád, otherwise called Kûtiáná. There is an exceedingly interesting Persian inscription in the Jammá Mosque here, dated Sûr Sun 940, equivalent to A. D. 1539, during the reign of Sûltán Mahomed III. of Gûjarát. This inscription declares the founder of the mosque to be one Ibrahim Nizám Jharumi or Nizámi in the reign of the greatest of Sûltáns Mahmûd Sháh, son of Latif Sháh, brother of Báhádursháh, son of Muzfarasháh, son of Mahumadsháh, son of Ahmedsháh, son of Muhammadsháh, son of Muzafarsháh. The tomb of Niámat Khán Lodhi is shown at the shrine of Pir Miskinsháh. It bears a short Persian inscription saying that Niámat Khán Lodhi drank the fatal draught of the cup bearer of death in the month of Rajab A. H. 1160, equivalent to A. D. 1747. A fair is held at this Pir's shrine on the Mahomedan festival of the Shûbibarát. The fair lasts for three days. A fair lasting for two days is also held at the temple of the Nágnáth Máhádev on the 7th and 8th of the dark half of the month of Shrávan. Excellent clothes for both men and women are made here; they are locally called Káchhás, Lûnghis, Dhotars, Mirkhánis, Gajiánis, and Aláyachás. Dyers also drive a flourishing trade here. Under Mûhammadan rule it grew into a town, and the local governor, one Kálidása, surrounded it with a fort. When the Moghal power no longer prevailed in the province, Kûtiáná fell into the hands of the local Mûhammadan garrison, who finally elected Niámat Khán Lodhi as their chief. Afterwards in A. D. 1750 they handed over the fort to Ráná Sultánji of Porbandar, but being dissatisfied with his rule, they again rebelled, and in A.D. 1759 betrayed the fort and town to one Háshim Khán, an adopted son of Nawáb Bahádûr Khán. Diwán Amarji, the celebrated Diwán of Júnágadh, conquered Kûtiáná from this person in A. D. 1770. Afterwards when the Nawáb was inimical to the family of the Diwán, his brother Govindji took shelter in Kûtiáná, and withstood the attacks of the Nawáb Hámid Khán for one month, after which peace was concluded. Subsequent to this the ex-minister Kalián Hirji seized on Kûtiáná, but was expelled by the Diwán Ranchodji (son of the great Diwán Amarji), who expelled him in A.D. 1802 on behalf of the Nawáb of Júnagádh, in whose hands it remains. Small boats can sail from Kûtiáná to Navi immediately after the rainy season.

Lodhwá.

This village lies about seven and a half miles to the east-south-east of Sútrápádá. The population, according to the census of 1872, was 1,473 souls, but this number diminished to 1,405 in 1881 after the famine of 1878-79. The population consists chiefly of Áhirs, with a fair sprinkling of other castes. Áhir Bháno Bhagwán of the Bholo tribe attained distinction in former times as having fought gallantly with Káthi Jodhá Dhánáni when in outlawry. There are many bardic verses about this, but it is a singular fact that these Áhirs claim their descent from the Jethwás, and are described in this poem as so descended. Thus in the following lines this Áhir is called the lord of Bardá, and also as Jethwá. This shows that the Jethwás origin probably is from the Mer clan, and that they are merely the Ráj Shákhá of that tribe. The lines are as follows :—

पारिसे बंधुके मदोने पाडिया धीग कोइ वेरीयां शरे आयो ॥
धणी बरडातणो करे धंधकारियो, आडिये भाण भगवान आयो ॥

The enemies were felled by volleys of musketry, certain strong men opposed them.

The Lord of Bardá uttered warlike shouts, Bhán Bhagwán now opposed them at close quarters.

हेडवां दळां ने जभा भागा हुवा, वांकडा जेठवा कियल वेरो ॥
घडो छांडी गया कैक धानाणिया, फरे नही लोठवे कदि फेरो ॥

Of the opposing army some were slain and some fled, the stern Jethwá dispersed their force.

Some of the Dhánánis quitted the field, never again to harass Lodhwá.

केहेनार काठीतणी जाव किं काटीयो, वराशक जागियो भाण बीजो ॥
लाज खोवा कज़ु जाव किं लोठवे, वेहद भोलाघेर थियो वीजा ॥

The Káthiáni says, wherefore Kathis are you going to Lodhwá to lose your honor.

Doubtless another Bhán Jethwá has arisen, or another hero named Vijo has been found in the house of the Bholá.

अडामूळ फटकमां काडि दिये जेठवो, जेठवो झाटका घणा जोडे ॥
कोदिया तणी कहे इम कामनी, सात खातणो अे साथे छोडे ॥

The Jethwá uproots every one in the battle. The Jethwá deals many sword-cuts.

The wives of the enemy say, he disperses the troops of our army.

जागियो लोढवे वांकडो जेठवो, डाकियल लोठवे अशो दीठो ॥
वेरीयां लोठवे न को आवे वळी, पवंगां लोठवे धविाळिये पीठो ॥

The stern Jethwá is aroused at Lodhwá; at Lodhwá such a demon has appeared.

Now no enemy will again trouble Lodhwá, for at Lodhwá Pitho has seized their horses.

NOTE.—There are some good salt works at Lodhwá, and one or two beautiful groves of mangoes and other trees.

MAJEVADI.

Majevaḍi is a walled town with an inner citadel, and is situated on the north bank of the river Úben. It was here that according to one legend Ránik Devḍi lived in the potter's house before her marriage with Rá Khengár. The population consists chiefly of Khojahs and Kanbis. It was formerly the head-quarters of a Mahál, but is now subordinate to Wadál. The population was 1,971 souls according to the census of 1872, and increased in 1881 to 2,162. In A.D. 1798 Amin Sáhib, son of Jamádár Hámid, an officer of the Gáekwár, cannonaded the fort until a heavy tribute was agreed upon, on receiving which he retired.

MÁLIÁ.

Máliá, situated on the bank of the river Megal, is the head-quarters of a mahál or revenue sub-division, and a Wahiwatdár or Revenue collector, and a 1st Class Magistrate reside here. Máliá is about eighteen or twenty miles north of Veráwal, and about 30 to 32 south of Júnágadh. The population was 2,417 souls, according to the census of 1872, and 2,555 according to that of 1881. Máliá is particularly famous as being the head-quarters of a curious tribe called Háttis, who intermarry with the Avartia

Káthis, as well as their own peculiar Ávartia Háttis, and also sometimes with Áhirs. As they are considered Shákháyat Káthis, they do not intermarry with the other Shákháyat tribes of Wálá, Khûmán, and Khâchar. Nevertheless they do not trace their origin from Verâwalji, the reputed ancestor of the other Shákháyat tribes, but claim descent from Khûmánsingh of Údaypûr, the reputed ancestor of the Jogiá Khûmáns. Hathisingh, the reputed ancestor of the Háttis, was brother to Jogáji, the founder of the Jogiá Khúmán tribe. They and two other brothers are said to have left Mewár and come to Sorath, and the following generations are given by the bards :—

KHÚMÁNSINGH.

Hathisingh.	Jogáji.	Mánsingh.	Katármal.

Hathisingh.
Khimánand.
Desûr.
Málo.
Áshait.
Khimánand.
Áshait.
Dosa.

Sharman.	Sájan.	Sagál.	Devo.
Máliá, Khorásá Láthodra, &c.	Kesod, &c.	Pánkhán, Eklerá, Shimroli, & Shilodar, &c.	Shergadh.

The descent from Khûmánsingh, and the generations previous to the four brothers last named, are probably imaginary, but these four brothers are no doubt the ancestors of the present Hattis, who probably really entered this province with the Jagatsingh, who conquered Wanthali from Rá Mandlik 1st in about A. D. 1270. We know from the Wanthali inscription that Jagatsingh's race held Wanthali for five generations, and that then it reverted to the Rás of Júnágadh. The Hattis were more fortunate and multiplied largely, and from Máliá and Kesod spread over a large tract of country as far as or futher than Kálej on the west and Kántrásá on the east—Máliá on the north and Mandor to the south. Eleven generations after Sharman of Máliá was Mándan Hátti, who had two sons, Sharman and Kálo. Sharman retained Máliá, Wadálá, Jánadi, Galodar, Bhandûri and Ghûnghati while Kálo went to Láthodrá. Thirteen generations after this Sharman, was Pálo, who had seven sons, of whom the eldest was Bhoj. Bhoj's descendants are the present grásiás of Máliá. Bhoj Hátti retained Máliá to the exclusion of his brethren who went to war with him, but were unable to oust him, and he retained the tálúkah, making after much fighting the concession of some grás to his brethren. As Bhoj's line was alone and the six brethren joined together to war with him, his line are called Pátlá (scanty) Háttis, while the offspring of his brethern are known as jádá (numerous) Háttis. At the present day, however, the Pátlá Háttis outnumber the jádá Háttis, and hold more grás. Bhoj built a tower in Máliá known as the Bhoj Kothá, and his son Devo is said to have built the Máliá fort. Bhoj's great-grandson was a famous warrior, called Pitháit, regarding whose exploits there are many bardic verses. He had a famous feud with the Ráizádahs of Chorwár, and when Kûnwar Bajiji and his uncle Sangji invaded the Máliá territory in about A. D. 1787, they were defeated and slain by the Háttis. But the Nawáb of Júnágadh shortly afterwards conquered Chorwár, and in 1795-96 reduced Máliá, when Pitháit Hátti surrendered the fort of Máliá, four villages and a half share of the town of Máliá was retained by him, the rest of the tâlûkah being annexed by Júnágadh. Dhanej is said to have been granted to Sájan Dhakel, an Avartia Hátti by one of the Chûdásama Rás of Júnágadh, for assistance given to him on the occasion of the siege and capture of Bet and Dwárká. Some of this man's descendants still hold land in Dhanej. The Háttis are called by the bards Mewádás, as though they came from Mewád (Mewar). There are about 500 or 600 houses of Háttis in the Júnágadh territory, some of which are in the Mángrol villages.

MÁNGAROL.

This city, the ancient Mangalapûr Pátan, is supposed by some to be the Monoglossum of Ptolemy. It is situated on the shore of the Arabian sea in about 70° 10′ East longitude and 21° 7′ North latitude. It was called by the Múhammadans Mangalûr or Mángalor, and this by a provincialism has been corrupted to Mángarol. As however there was another Mangalûr in the Konkan, this Mangalûr was called by seamen by way of distinction, Sorathi Mangalûr while that was called Malabári Mangalûr or Konkani Mangalûr. This distinction accounts for the Surati Maugalor of Barbosa and other old travellers. The first ruling race here of whom we have any records is the Gohil, mentioned in an inscription of great interest dated Samwat 1202, A. D. 1146, *i.e.* during the reign of Kûnwár Pál of Anhilwádá Pátan. This, after reciting the supreme power of Sidhráj Jayasingh and his succession by Kûnwár Pál, relates that Sahár of the Gohil race ruled there, and that his son Sahjig obscurod the glory of the Choulûkyas and that his sons were powerful protectors of the country of Sauráshtra; of these sons, Mûlûk was the elder, and Somráj, the younger. Somráj in memory of his father erected the templo of Sahjigeshwar at Mángarol, and placed a pinnacle on the temple of Somnáth at Pátan. His elder brother Mûlûk, who is styled Náyak of Sauráshtra set apart certain levies for the maintenance of the temple at Mángarol, Wámansthali, Chorwad, Láthodrá, Walejá and Talásbhávya, and gave also an irrigated field at Visanwel, and certain rights on salt at Mángalor. I am totally unable to give any further particulars about these Gohils beyond the fact that the Mandlika Kávya speaks of them as being Surya Vamsi and they were probably cadets of the Gohilots of Valabhi. Colonel Tod, indeed, speaks of the Gohils of Div, but quotes no authority. Sahjig possibly founded the Shri Singh era, as he appears to have successfully asserted his independence against the Choulûkyas. This era is mentioned in the inscription, which was inscribed in the year 32 of the Shri Singh era, so the era may date either from Sahár's or Sahjig's accession. Subsequently we hear of Bhán Jethwá's rule here, and that he gave in marrige here 1800 virgins in order to be permitted to take back a favourite wife whom he had divorced, and he built a grand nuptial hall at Mángarol for this occasion. This was subsequently cast down by Shams-ud-din Anwar Khán, locally called Shams Khán, the viceroy of Ṣûltán Firoz Tûghlak, and built up into the Jamá mosquo by Iz-ûd-din bin Áram Sháh, the local governor in the reign of the same Sûltán, A. H. 775., A.D. 1373. The inscription in the Sodhiwáo shows that this well was built in St. 1375, equivalent to A.D. 1319, in the reign of Ráûl Shri Mahipaldeva, but it is difficult to say whether this Mahipal was a Gohil or a Chuḍásama. A Chuḍásama of this name was no doubt reigning at this time, but it is quite possible that the name Mahipal may have been borne by a Gohil, and the title Ráûl is a Gohil and not a Chuḍásama title. From the Kodinar inscription of St. 1328, A.D. 1272, one Gand Shri Virbhadra is said to have given to Nágar Nána a seventh share in Mángarol. Probably he was a descendant of Bháo Brihaspati, who was stationed at Pátan by Kûmárpála of Anhilwádá. After Bhán Jethwâ it is difficult to say who ruled at Mángarol, but possibly the Chávadás or Wájás of Pátan either governed it direct or else through some local vassal, probably a Wághelá, and connection of the Dholká Wághelás. Ranchoḍji Diwán says distinctly Wághelás, and I incline to think that the Rájá Jayapál, who is described in the ballad of the fall of Pátan as having married the sister of the Chávadá rájá Kûnwarpál of Pátan, may have been a Wághelá. The ballad, indeed, says distinctly that he was a Wágher, but *r* and *l* are interchangeable, and the ballad is written in the Persian character. Mángarol doubtless came under the Múhammadan yoke from the commencement of the 14th century, together with the rest of Nágher, and the frequent inscriptions show that rule to have been, at least from the time of the emperor Firoz Tûghlak, continuous. There is another inscription in the Ráwali mosque of the reign of this emperor, viz., A. H. 780, and yet another in the Rahmat mosque of A.H. 784. There is yet another even more interesting as being dated A. H. 797 and bearing the name of Sháh-in-Sháh Nûsrat Jahán Badsháh, whose chief vazir or viceroy is said to be Mûsafar Zûfar Khan. This inscription is bilingual, and the Sanscrit version says distinctly that it was inscribed in Samvat 1452 and in the reign of Pádsháh Sri Nûsrat, and it states that his viceroy Jáfar Khán was ruling in Gújarát on his behalf, and that Rái Mûltáni Vairshi's son Malik Yákûb was a pearl merchant there: that Malik Mûsa was kotwál of Mángarol, and that doors faced with iron were at this time fitted into the gateways. This is the Nûsrat Sháh of Mr. Thomas, (see his Prinsep, Vol. II., p. 311). Another interesting inscription is dated Samvat 800 at the time of Timûr's invasion. This mentions that Khán Ázam Zúfar Khán Wajih was ruling with entire power in Gújarát, that this viceroy in Sorath was Malik Badar Banjhal, and his deputy in Mángarol Malik Shekh bin Táj, and that he built a fort round the town. There is yet another without date in the reign of Násir-úd-dûnya wa-ûd-din Ábul Fateh Áhmed Sháh, during the viceroyalty of Prince Fateh Khán, and afterwards another showing that in A.H. 1047 (A.D. 1637) in the reign of the emperor Sháh Jahán, Jamál Khán Loháni who held Mángarol in jagir, built at that place a serái. There is one more worthy of notice as it shows that Mángarol fell into the hands of the Peshwa, and that his Lieutenant was expelled after holding the town twelve years by Shaháb-úd-din and Shekh Fakhar-úd-din in A.H. 1162 (A.D. 1748). Fakhar-úd-din was an ancestor of the present Shekhs of Mángarol. From this date Mángrol was held by the Sheikhs. In A.D. 1764 in the time of Sheikh Mian, son of Fakhar-ûd-din, Diwán Amarji attacked Mángarol on behalf of Nawáb Mahábat Khán I. of Júnágadh, and compelled him to yield to that chieftain a half share in his paraganah. Since this date Mángarol has owned more or less the authority of Júnágadh, which has been confirmed by the British Government. Mángarol used to be a port of some consequence, but owing to various causes does now but little trade; Barbosa speaks of its exporting horses, wheat, rice, cotton cloths, vegetables, &c. Now its trade is principally confined to local wants. It is famous for the inlaid ivory and carved sandalwood boxes (also made at Surat) which are usually known as Bombay work. They are exported to Bombay and sold there. Near Mángarol is the shrine of Syad Sikandar, a Tirmizi Syad, who accompanied

Shams Khán's army, and who was a companion of Sikandar Khán, who was left there as thánahdár by him (Tarikh-i Sorath). A memo. drawn up by Syad Áhmad and sent me by Mr. Campbell, says that Syad Sikandar commanded a force sent with him under Iz-ûd-din, and that at this time a Hindû named Kûnwarpál governed Mángarol. The Rájá not accepting Islám was slain in battle, and Syad Sikandar took possession of the country, but appointed Iz-ûd-din as the governor thereof, and himself retired to Dewalpûr. The date given for the capture of Mángarol is A.H. 770 (A.D. 1368). This date is probably correct. The memo. says that Iz-ûd-din after allotting this village to the Syad returned to Delhi, but the inscription of A.H. 775 shows that he was still then local governor. Probobly Syad Sikandar merely accompanied Shams Khan's expedition, and was left here with Iz-ûd-din, who was directed to allot him maintenance. But as a local saint, Syad Sikandar in later times got the credit of the conquest. This would appear also from an inscription of A.H. 1162. There are numerous relics at the shrine, amongst which are a rosary and handkerchief said to have belonged to the Virgin Mary. There is an amusing story told about a cup in the possession of the Syad's descendants, which he is said to have wrested from an angel. The population of Mángarol, according to the census of 1872, was 15,341 souls, but in 1881 sank to 12,123 after the famine of 1878-79. The ironsmiths of Mángarol are famous for their skill. Mángarol is also famous for its musk-melons. The celebrated Diwán Amarji of Júnágadh was born at this town. The shrine of Kámnáth Máhádeva is situated about five miles to the east of Mángarol, and many vows are made to the god. On the 15th of the light half of the month of Kártik and the last day of the dark half of the month of Srávana, a fair is held here. There is a well lying to the north of the town of Mángarol at a distance of about, 200 yards, the land surrounding this well forms a tract of about five or six miles in circumference, and is called Lábûr Kûá after this well. Excellent cotton is grown in this land, and is called Lábûr-Kûa cotton, and finds a ready sale in the Bombay market. There is a Goverument vernacular school, as well as a girls' school at Mángarol. There is a post-office in Mangarol and the Saurashtra post also comes to Mángarol viá Sil. New plantations of betel vines have lately been started at Mangarol.

Nágasari.

This village is situated about ten miles to the west of Bherái, and four miles north of Jáfarábád. Nágasari was formerly called Nágpûr-Pátan, and occupied a site about 600 yards to the south-west of the present village on the opposite bank of the Ráidi stream. There are several ruined wells with steps (*wávs*) near here. Coins are found on this old site in the rainy season. The population of Nágasari, according to the census of 1872, was 1,668, and according to that of 1881 was 1,865 souls. It is mentioned as a bárah or roadstead in the Mirat-i-Ahmadi, though in fact it does not correspond to the definition of a bárah as given in that work. Probably it was formerly connected with the Jáfarábád creek, and that town may have been the port, and Nágasari inland market town (Kasbah). Rûkhaḍ Warú, a Bábriá, flourished about a century ago, and was renowned for his prowess. In bardic poetry he is styled Lord of Bardá, and is said to have preserved the food and water of the Paraj or Káthis. There seems in truth to be very little difference between Káthis, Bábriás, Áhirs, Mehars and Mhyas, and in all probability the name Jethwá is merely Jyesth or Jesht, *i.e.*, chief, that is to say they are the Rájkúla of the Mers. The Ain-i-Akbari notices this similarity, and says that the Káthis are by caste Áhirs. This Rûkhaḍ's mother was named Dholi, and was so famous, that he is not known by his father's name, but his mother's, and is called by the bards "Son of Dholi." It is a saying among Hindus "Whose mother can have eaten a sir (pound) of ginger?" Alluding to the custom of women being given ginger with other restoratives after their confinement. The saying means, who is there strong enough to eat a pound of ginger? But with regard to Dholi, she is said to have eaten a pound of ginger when Rûkhaḍ was born, hence it was not wonderful that the son of such a mother should be a mighty hero. There is a Government vernacular school and a branch Post-office at Nágasari. The inhabitants of Nágasari reverence Shámji Mahárάj of Tûlsishâma as their tutelary god.

PASNÁVADÁ.

This village is situated five and a half miles to the east of Sûtrápádá, and the inhabitants are principally of the Jádav, Bárad, Ráthod, Chohán, Vais, Dodia, Nukûm clans, and other Kárdiá Rájpûts. According to the census of 1872 the population amounted to 1,230 souls, but after the famine of 1878-79 it sank to 1,163 persons in all. There is a temple and kûnd or reservoir here sacred to Gáyatri, the wife of Bramhá. I am not aware of any other temple in India sacred to this goddess. The ruins at Pasnávadá show it to have been once a large and populous place. The inscription of Samvat 1514 / A.D. 1458 is a singularly interesting, both as being bilingual (Persian and Sanskrit), and as showing that in A. D. 1458 Pasnávadá was governed by Malik Asad, son of Malik Muhammad, son of Malik Mûbárak, on behalf of Sûltan Kûtbûddin of Gûjarát. This local official caused the fort wall to be built.

PRÁCHI KÚND.

Práchi Kûnd, about fifteen miles east of Pátan, is situated on the bank of the Sarasvati river at the point where this river takes a turn towards the east (Prách), and hence is called Práchi. The original Práchi is said to have been at the village of Ájotá, about eight miles to the west of the present Práchi. There are two kûnds or reservoirs in the river-bed, where it thus turns to the east. These kûnds are held to be very sacred, and they who perform a pilgrimage here, bathe therein. There is a Pipal tree at Práchi, known as the Moksh Pipal, so called because the sight of it is supposed to deliver those who are possessed by Bhûts from these demons. They who are possessed come hither and are here delivered from the Bhûts. They who are childless also come hither and worship their ancestors, &c., here, in the hopes of being blessed with offspring. The three days, 13th, 14th, and 15th of the light half of the months of Kártik, Chaitra and Shrávan, are called Práchi days, because on these days ceremonies performed at Práchi are more efficacious. The principal worship conducted at Práchi is that of ancestors. In another small kûnd in the river is an image of Vishnû, about four feet high, which is immersed to the waist in water, and is held very sacred, and it is called Práchi Mádhava. Pilgrims pay their adorations here. There are large assemblies of pilgrims here in the Práchi days of Kártik and Chaitra, and the Nawáb Sáhib levies a toll of eight annas per head from each pilgrim. There are two dharamsálás at Práchi kûnd, one built by Vithal Ráo Dewáji, the famous Sûbahdár of the Gáekwar, and the other by the Júnágadh Darbár. It is said that the Pándavs were advised to go and bathe in Práchi Sarasvati by Krishna, who told Yûdishthir that it was more sacred than Gayáji, the Ganges and Pûshkar. On the bank of this river is the temple of the Batheshwar Máhádeva, of which the emblem or linga is very large. Barren women make vows to this god to make certain offerings if they should bear a child. Then they come and embrace the linga. People believe that if they are able to embrace the linga properly they will be made fruitful.

Phúlká.

This village lies about twelve miles to the north-west of the town of Úná. The population in 1872 amounted to 272, but sank in 1881 to 207 souls after the famine of 1878-79. It was formerly a mere nes or hamlet, and was repeopled in $\frac{\text{St. 1858}}{\text{A.D. 1862}}$ by Koli Vejá Káná. The population consists at present principally of Áhirs, and Sorathiá Talpadá and Ghediá Kolis, Sindhis and Wájá Rájpûts. There is a very interesting Pályo or funeral monument here of one Lákhá, son of Sáyá of the Masáhani tribe, who built a temple on the bank of the Phûlká Taláo. It is dated $\frac{\text{St. 1418}}{\text{A.D. 1392}}$ in the reign of the victorious Shivgan. This Shivgan is evidently the same as the Shivgan of the Bhûwátimbi inscription, and was probably one of the Wájá Rájás of Somnáth who ruled the coast line from Mádhavpûr to Jáfarábád. This coast line is usually called Nágher. Another ancient memorial-stone, dated $\frac{\text{St. 1475}}{\text{A.D. 1119}}$, shows that one Parmár Ráj Kashiá, son of Parmár Márû Hariá, was killed while defending the village and protecting cows and women. Vahi or Dhárá Bandar lies about twenty-six miles south of the village. The tank contains water all the year round, and is about 90 paces in length by 70 in breadth. It is covered with weeds and rushes.

Rámpúrá.

This village is three miles south south-west of Bherái. The population in 1872 was 784, but diminished in 1881 to 663, consequent on the famine of 1878-79. The deserted site of the old village of Malikpûr is situated near the present village of Rámpûrá, and is said to have been the seat of a Rájpût chief. There is a Sati's memorial-stone near the site of Malikpûr, about which they say that it is the memorial-stone of Bráhmani, who immolated herself alive on the funeral pile, because the Rájá persecuted her husband and endeavoured to levy taxes from his land. Before mounting the funeral pile, the Sati cursed the chief, and he was shortly slain and his capital became a ruin. Rampûrá is said to have successfully withstood two attacks—first when Lomá and Virá of the Wágh clan of Áhirs repulsed an armed band from the village of Mûndiá. A local poem commemorates this exploit, and styles these brethren as sons of Hádá and grandsons of Kûmbhá. Afterwards, when the Khûmáns of Chhelna and Bhamodrá attacked Rámpûrá, they were beaten off with much loss by Jamádárs Laving and Abdûlláh. The Júnágadh Darbár rewarded those Jamádárs handsomely on this occasion. Jamádár Laving had a daughter named Rahmatbái, who married a husband named Yakûb. Her son Áhmad is alive at this day. There is an old temple of the Cháchûdá Mahádeva on a height overlooking the sea. The lands of Rampûrá reach the sea-shore and are immediately opposite to the Shiál island. The river Dhántarwadi flows near the village and retains water throughout the entire year. Another deserted site called Múlwadar is to be found in the lands of Rámpûrá. The population of Rámpûrá consists chiefly of Áhirs. The Dhántarwadi river flows into the sea just below the head land which is crowned by the temple of the Cháchûdá Mahádeva.

Ránpúr.

Ránpúr, about twelve miles to the N. E. from Júnágadh, is

the seat of the branch of the Bábi family sprung from Mùzafar Khán and Fatehyáb Khán. These persons rebelled against the Nawáb Mahábat Khán 1st, but were worsted. Eventually on condition of resigning all claims to the gádi they received Ránpúr in jágir. These Bábis are not of the Júnágadh line. They are the offspring of Sher Khán, *brother* of Salábat Khán, while the Júnágadh line are the offspring of Sher Khán, *son* of Salábat Khán. Ránpúr is situated on the bank of the Úben river, and the climate is good. The population, according to the census of 1872, was 2,132 souls, and increased in 1881 to 2,700.

Rohisá.

This village is situated about eight miles to the east of the town of Úná, and about half a mile from the sea-shore. The population, according to the census of 1872, was 995, and according to that of 1881, 869 souls. This diminution is due to the famine of 1878-79. The population consists chiefly of Wájá Rájpûts, Bháts, and others. It was here at Rohisá that the famous Úgá Wálá was slain by order of Rá Kawát of Júnágadh, and his memorial-stone stands to this day on the Chitrásar boundary. This memorial-stone does not exactly face the east, as is the invariable custom, but is bending forward. It is said that Úgá Wálá's sister came to visit her brother's memorial-stone, but could not distinguish which was his out of the group at this spot. In her grief she implored her brother to give some sign which was his memorial-stone, and on this Wálá Úga's pályo is said to have bent forward in her direction as though to greet her. It is still in this position. In former times the Gáriádhár chieftain's maternal uncle lived at Rohisá, and endeavoured to conquer Gariádhár. Hence the Gáriádhár chieftain took an oath never to mount the gádi until he had conquered Rohisá, but he never was able to do so; hence in order to keep his oath, a stone was brought from Rohisá at the time he ascended the gádi as a token that Rohisá was conquered, though in fact this was not the case. Ever since this when a Pálitáná chieftain mounts the gádi, a stone is brought from Rohisá. Ladho Wájo is said to have brought a large stone hither from Gáriádhár, and this stone is built into the raised platform in front of the Chorá, or village guest-house. The Chitrásar lake lies about three miles to the north of Rohisá. The legend about it is very curious. It is said that a strange merchant came to trade at Rohisá with an exceedingly intelligent dog called Chitro. He purchased goods to a large amount from a Wániá on credit, and when asked for security, offered to leave his dog. The Wániá agreed, and the stranger departed, having strictly enjoined his dog not to leave the Wániá until he should return. The dog stayed accordingly, and soon became a universal favourite. After a month or two a burglary was committed at the Wániá's house and much property was carried off, but Chitro made signs to the people to follow him, and led them into the jungle to a spot where he stopped and began to scratch. The Wánia had the ground dug up and found all his stolen property. On this he was very much pleased, and declared that the dog had defrayed his master's debt. He wrote therefore a receipt for the money due to him by the stranger and an account of what had happened, and tied it round the dog's neck and told him to go and seek his master. The dog set out, but had not gone many miles when he met his old master who was on his way to Rohisá to pay his debt. His master, seeing his dog coming in the distance, thought he had been faithless and had left the Wániá. When the dog came up to him, he cursed him and said, "Thou wast faithless, but I came." On hearing this reproach the dog fell dead. His master now for the first time perceived the note tied to his neck, and reading it, understood how nobly the dog had behaved and how unworthily he had rewarded him for his goodness. Then he wept bitterly, and caused the Chitrásar lake to be excavated and built round at the spot where the dog fell dead, and he built a temple on the little island in the lake, in which he placed the dog's image, which is there to this day. Afterwards a village was founded near the tank, which was called Chitrásar also after this small lake.

Sháná Caves.

The Sháná hill is sixteen miles north of Úná one mile north of Vánkia, and ten miles south-west of Dedán; close to the hill flows the Rupen river. There are about 60 caves in all, and there was evidently a large and flourishing monastery here. The caves are well supplied with little tanks of water and the architecture is very simple, there being scarcely any tracery or ornamentation in any of the caves. There are no inscriptions, hence it is difficult to assign an exact date to these caves, but they probably belong to the same period as those of Talájá.

Sásan.

Sásan is a small hamlet or village on the southern bank of the Hiran river. It is the head-quarters of the Superintendent of the Gir Forest. Sásan means punishment in Sanskrit, and probably the name is derived from the fact that in ancient times state prisoners were sent here and to Chhelna in order that they might die quickly from the poisonous quality of the water. In front of this village and on the northern bank of the Hiran is the Wánsádhol hill, which is a conspicuous feature in the Northern Gir. In the Northern Gir the most famous hill is that called Chánchái in Amreli territory. Locally it is called the Charkálo, and is the highest hill in the province after the Girnár and Dátar hills. It is 2,128 feet above the sea. In the south-eastern Gir there is another lofty hill, called Nándi velo, 1,741 feet above the sea level. It is a land-mark in clear weather to ships making the Káthiawár Coast.

Pátan Somnáth.

This celebrated city, situated in about 23° 53' North latitude and 70° 24' East longitude, is usually called Pátan Somnáth, Prabhás-Pátan, Dewa-Pátan, and in modern times Verávwal-Pátan. It is the chief town of that portion of the coast belt called Nágher, extending from Mádhavpûr under Porbandar to the further frontier of Bábriáwár. This portion of the coast appears to have been highly cultivated and populous from the earliest times, and to have carried on trade with the Red Sea, Persian Gulf, and African Coast, as well as with other Indian ports. It was celebrated as being the city of the famous shrine of Somnáth. This is the place where the Jádavs slew each other, and where Krishna was shot by the Bhil. The three rivers, Sarasvati, Hiranya, and Kapilá, unite near here, and form the sacred Triveni ere they join the boundless ocean. The following description of the site is borrowed from the Rás Málá:—"The "small port and bay of Veráwal lie on the south-western cost of "Saurashtrá, in a country exceedingly rich, thickly wooded and "in high cultivation. Upon a projection of land, forming the "southern extremity of this little bay, which with its bold and "graceful curvature, and its golden sands kept in perpetual "agitation by the surf, has been pronounced unrivalled in India, "stands the city of Dev Pátan or Prabhâs." It appears from the first accounts which can now be gleaned, whether of history or tradition, to have been ruled by the Chávadâs, and the almost unanimous consensus of ancient writers, declares its shores to have been infested by pirates. Marco Polo alone speaks of its being a place of considerable trade and free from corsairs, but this is not the view taken by Al Birûni or indeed by other writers. Mahmûd of Ghazni conquered the town in A D. 1024, and it certainly appears both from legends, ballads, and the testimony of inscriptions that he left behind a Múhammadan Governor. Subsequently the Wájás (a sub-branch of the Ráthod tribe) acquired Somnáth Pátan and the kingdom of Nágher, and revived the glories of the ancient fane. But it was again cast down by Álagh Khán circa A.D. 1300, and the coast belt or Nágher kingdom conquered. From this date Múhammadan supremacy prevailed throughout the belt, and from the reign of Muhammad Tughlak regular governors were appointed. The inscriptions of the time of the emperor Firoz Tughlak show a settled dominion, and this continued throughout the time of the Gûjarát Sûltáns, both anterior and posterior to the conquest of Júnágadh by Mahmûd Begadha. Previous to Álagh Khán's conquest we find local chieftains ruling at Pátan subject to the paramount power of the Anhilwádá sovereigns. Subsequently we find local chieftains owning the sway of Delhi. Then the Gûjarát Sûltáns became paramount, and finally Pátan fell under the Moghals after the conquest of Sorath in Akbar's reign. By this time the temple had again been levelled twice, viz., once by

Mûzafar 1st, and once by his grandson, Áhmad Sháh 1st of Gûjarát, and the local chieftains were effaced. Afterwards when the Moghal power was dissolved, Pátan was usurped by the Kasbátis, and was conquered at different times by the Shekh of Mángrol and the Ráná of Porbandar; but finally, owing to the gallantry and statesmanship of Diwán Amarji, it was conquered by the Nawáb of Júnágadh in whose hands it remains. Barbosa (Stanley's translation) spoaks of Patemxi or Pátan Shri as a great city, a good seaport, very rich, and of great trade. In point of fact Pátan has been and has remained populous, principally owing to two causes. The first was its fame as a shrine, and this attracted hither thousands of visitors and pilgrims from all parts of India up till about the middle of the fifteenth century, and when the shrine had been ruined past recognition, and when consequently its populousness would have suffered, it had become the principal port of embarkation for Múhammadan pilgrims to the cities of Makkah and Madinah, and this lasted until it was superseded by Surat. Though it is eclipsed now as far as wealth and population are concerned, by the neighbouring and immediately adjacent port of Verâwal, it is still an important town. The population of Pátan by the census of 1872 was 6,856, and in 1881 this number fell to 6,644 owing to the ravages of the famine of 1878-79. The rule of the Chúḍásamás never appears to have extended to Pátan and Nágher, which seems, until the Múhammadan conquest, to have been ruled by local chieftains. Somnáth is said to have been called Bhairaveshwar in the Satya Yûg, Shrávarnikeshwar in the Treta Yûg, Shrigáleshwar in the Dwápûr Yûg, and in the present or Kali Yûg, Somnáth. The temple is said to have been first built of gold by Somráj, then of silver by Rávana, then of wood by Krishna, and then of stone by Bhimdova of Anhilwádá, and to have been repaired and beautified by Kumárpála of Anhilwádá. Ahilya Bái, widow of Holkar, built the new temple of Somnáth at a little distance from the old one in A.D. 1783.

Pátan, called in Sanskrit Pattan, is the capital of the division of the peninsula called the Prabhása Kshetra. Prabhása means the very shining, the exceedingly brilliant. The Prabhása

Khanda or Prabhása chapter of the Skanda Púrána contains many shlokas or verses as to the reason why this country and town were named Prabhása. It would be too long to quote them all, but I quote three as being specially interesting.

प्रथम भासितं देवि सर्वेषा भुवी तेजसोः ॥
तीर्था नामादि तीर्थे यत् प्रभासंतंन कीर्तितं ॥

Oh! goddess of all the splendid places on earth, this is the most brilliant. It is the first of places of pilgrimage, hence it is called Prabhás.

अथवा दक्षशपेन, चेंदुना निःप्रभेणच ॥
तत्र देवि प्रभा लब्धा, तेन प्राभासिकं स्मृतं ॥

Oh! goddess, the brilliancy which the moon lost from the curse of Daksha.
Here it recovered, and therefore is this place called Prabhás.

प्रत्यक्षं भास्करो यत्र, सदातिष्ठ तिभामिनि ॥
तेन प्रभास नामेति, त्रिषु लोकेषु विश्रुतं ॥

Oh wife! The place where the sun is always present,
Is on that account called Prabhása in the three worlds.

The story of Daksha is as follows: Daksha was a demigod created by Brahmá for the purpose of creating animal and vegetable life. He had fifty daughters, of whom he married twenty-seven, who now shine in heaven as the twenty-seven lunar mansions (nakshatras) to the moon. But the moon loved Rohini (the asterism in Taurus consisting of 5 stars and including the bright star Aldebáran) alone and remained solely with her. On this the other twenty-six damsels complained to their father, and Daksha scolded the moon and desired him to treat his wives equally. But the moon remained obdurate: on which Daksha cursed him and doomed him to suffer from perpetual consumption. The moon, stricken with grief, now sought all the holy places for alleviation of his pain, and after visiting many places in vain, at length came to Prabhása, where he worshipped Shiva with great devotion. Shiva, taking pity on him, directed that he should wane in brilliancy for 15 days, but in the following 15 days should recover his lost splendor. In gratitude for this, the moon erected a golden temple to Shiva over the previously existing linga, and named it Somnáth or Lord of the Moon, in memory of the service rendered him. The linga at Somnáth is one of the 12 famous so called self-existent lingas, not installed or established by any one. The temple, though as above mentioned three times destroyed by the Múhammadans, was nevertheless three times rebuilt, and so late as A. D. 1700 was still a place of great sanctity. But in 1706 Aurangzeb ordered its destruction, and looking at the style in which the ruins have been patched up, and the poorness of the remains, there seems every reason to believe that this order was carried out. The Prabhása Kshetra is also called the Bháskara Kshetra, and this term also seems, like the third Shloka above quoted, to allude to the ancient worship of the sun formerly so prevalent throughout the coast belt, and especially in Nágher. Another name of Pátan is Shiva Pattan, but this name occurs principally in bardic verse, see Rás Málá edition of 1878 (page 276). The limits of the Prabhása Kshetra are given in the following Shloka :

पुर्वे तप्तोदक : स्वामी, पश्चिमे माधव : स्मृत ॥
उतरे सुर्य पुत्रीच, दाक्षिणे सरिता पत्ति ॥

On the east Taptodaka Swámi; on the west, they say, is Mádhav ; on the north the daughter of the Sun ; and on the south the lord of the rivers. Taptodaka Swami is Tûlsishâma. Madhava is the shrine of Krishna, Madhava Rái at Mádhavapûr. The daughter of the Sun is the Bhadrávati, or river Bhádar, and the lord of the rivers is the sea. One of the legends in the Púránas relative to the old Sun worship in Pattan is as follows. Súrya Náráyana (the sun) used formerly to shine in Prabhása—with his full splendour. This was so great that his wife Chháya (shadow) could not approach him, he therefore divided his brilliancy into sixteen parts and retained only four, *i. e.*, one-fourth of the whole, and thus Chháya was able to come near her husband, from whom she is inseparable. The remaining 12 sixteenths of his brilliancy he bestowed on 12 temples of the Sun in Prabhás Kshetra. Pátan seems to have been the head-quarters of the Wájá rule, though the Chûḍásamás territory reached as near as Goraj about six miles north of Mángrol, where there is a Pályo or memorial stone dated $\frac{\text{St. 1150}}{\text{A.D. 1394}}$ to the memory of Patel Pûná's son Bhima, who fell fighting in the reign of in the victorious reign of Mokalsingh while rescuing the village cattle. The concluding words of the inscription are confused, but there is distinct mention of the Wájá frontier. The following is an extract from the inscription dated $\frac{\text{St. 1225}}{\text{A. D. 1169}}$ in the temple of the Bhadra Káli goddess :—

महो वदन पंकजं भुवन —— भूषा विधि
निधि : सकळ संपदां त्रिपुर वेरिण : संमतं ॥
तदे तद तिदु : सहेक्षय विनास सिद्धो पुरा
शशांक रचितं पुरं जयति वारिये : सन्निधौ : ॥९॥

This city, as it were the face (*i. e.*, the most beautiful part) of the earth, the ornament of the world, and treasury of all wealth, specially favoured by Mahádeva, was established by the moon to celebrate the cure of his grievous malady of consumption, and stands in a commanding position near the sea.

Somnáth Pattan is also called Sompûr, and hence the Sompura Bráhmans and masons derive their names. It is said that these masons (Saláts) were originally Bráhmans, and the caste were seated at dinner on the seashore on the occasion of the installation of the Bhidiá Mahádeva or Shashi Bhûshan Mahádeva between Pattan and Verávval. (This temple was said to have been originally built by the moon.) On this occasion a fish fell into the vessel in which the food was being cooked, and they who partook of this food became Sompura Saláts (or masons) while they who abstained, remained Sompurá Bráhmans. It is said that the moon brought these Bráhmans with him, and they asked him what provision he was going to make for them. He replied that they should be the priests of this only place of pilgrimage. Since then they have remained here as priests of this shrine and are called Sompurás. The Sompurá masons are however no longer to be found in Pattan, but some still live in Dhrángadhrá, Visalnagar, &c.

Sultán Mahmúd's celebrated expedition appears to have been made in A.D. 1026; he seems to have marched with such rapidity by way of Anhilwárá Pátan that the Hindû Rájás were unable to collect their forces for its defence. Thence he seems to have marched by way of the Bhál, *i.e.*, the country between Wadhwán and Walá to the sea coast, and to have destroyed Delwádá (Dabalwárah Elliot's India, Vol. II., p. 470), and thence to have marched upon Somnáth, and after a sharp fight for two days to have conquered both the city and temple, immense spoil was found in the temple, and after a short stay Mahmûd returned to Ghazni. Elliot (Vol. II., p. 472) says that ten thousand populated villages were held by the temple as an endowment and that three hundred musicians and five hundred dancing girls were attached to it. There were also 300 barbers to shave the heads of the pilgrims. In the account of the temple given in the 3rd Vol. of the Mirat-i-Áhmadi the destruction of the temple in the time of Aurangzeb is specially noted. From the above legends and accounts I think we may gather this much that the portion of the coast near Somnáth was in very ancient times specially famous for temples of the Sun and the country was ruled by a Solar dynasty, probably the Gohils. Afterwards a Chief of Lunar race named Somráj, possibly a Chávadá, conquered the country and erected the temple to Mahádeva calling it after his own name Somnáth. This has been explained in the Puránas by the legends above recounted. The temple at its most flourishing period may possibly have been endowed with 1,000 villages, but 10,000 seems out of the question.

Pátan is now specially famous for the manufacture of door-locks made of wood and iron. It is the head-quarters of a mahál or revenue division, and a revenue and judicial officer have their courts here. There is also a dispensary and vernacular school, and also a girls' school. The town is surrounded by a wall with towers at intervals and by a ditch, and there are some wealthy bankers and merchants residing there. But the monied classes have principally betaken themselves to the neighbouring town and port of Verával. Among the Múhammadan Saints the Mangroli Sháh is the most famous. He is said to have visited the town before its conquest by Mahmúd Ghaznavi, and to have been so disgusted at the oppression practised there, especially on the Mûhammadan population, that he journeyed to Ghazni and induced Sultán Mahmûd to effect the conquest of the place. His shrine is without the Veráwal gate of the city not far distant from the temple of the Bhidiá Mahádeva, and three fairs are held here during the year. (1.) That of Chánd-katál on the 16th of the Múhammadan month of Muharram at the shrine of Chánd-katál, about four miles to the north of the town. (2.) That of Mángroli Sháh in the month of Jeshta (June). (3.) The Daserá fair in the month of Áshvin Sud 10th, held in honour of the Kankái Mother.

The following Shloka is said about Prabhása Kshetra, but is also applied to Sorath, but the limits of Prabhása Kshetra closely or nearly correspond to those of the modern Sorath :—

प्रभासे पंच रत्नानि नदी नारी तुरंगमा : ॥
चतुर्थ : सोमनाथश्च, पंचमं हरि दर्शनम् : ॥

Prabhása has jewels five.
The river (Sarasvati) women, horses.
The fourth Somnáth, the fifth the presence of Hari.*

SÚTRÁPÁDÁ.

Sûtrápádá (originally Saptapáta or the town with seven separate quarters) has still seven separate quarters. It is the chief town of a mahál or revenue sub-division of the Júnágadh State, and is the head-quarters of a Wahiwatdár or revenue officer and a 2nd Class Magistrate. There is also a Post-office here. It is situated on the shore of the Arabian Sea, about seven miles S. E. of Pátan Somnáth. By the road it is even further, as the river of Pátan flows between. There is a reservoir here called the Chyavan Kûnda, sacred to Chyavan Rishi, who was the son of Bhrigu Rishi, who resided here with his wife Pûlomá, who was very beautiful. A Rákshas became enamoured of her. Her

* This alludes to Madhavapur, which is the limit of Prabhás Kshetra on the sea coast to the north-west.
FOOT NOTE.—He who has the moon as his ornament.

husband had gone to bathe in the Práchi reservoir, leaving her in charge of Agni. The Rákshas now entered the house, and in spite of the prohibition of Agni, forcibly carried her off. She implored the aid of Vishnu, who suddenly appeared and killed the Rákshas. At the time of her being carried off she was pregnant, and from her terror she had a premature delivery of a child, who on this account was called Chyavan. He afterwards became a great sage or Rishi, and was seated at the site of the present Chyavan Kùnd, performing religious austerities. These he performed so rigorously that a white ants' hill was formed over him. Rájá Sharyáti, son of Vaivaswat Manu, with his wife and daughter Sûkanyá, arrived here with all his retinue while hunting. His daughter with her maidens was strolling along the seashore and saw the ant-hill, and saw something shining inside and pushed in a stalk of grass. When she pulled out the stalk, it was stained with blood. She became alarmed, and ordered her maidens to pull down the ant-hill. They did so, and the Rishi was discovered much attenuated by his penance and deprived of both his eyes by the pushing in of the grass stalk. Sûkanyá begged for forgiveness, alleging that she was not aware of his being concealed there; and declared that she would marry him and take care of him. The Rishi replied that he was old and withered, and that she had better marry some handsome young Prince; but she refused to leave him. In the meantime, owing to the sin committed by her, her parents and their attendants all fell sick, and a servant came running to tell her that her parents were dying and that she must hasten if she wished to see them alive. She replied that she could not leave the Rishi, who, moved at her constancy, at once cured the whole party and her parents now married her to him, and purchasing the site of Sûtrápádá, then called Sûryapûr, bestowed it on her husband in dowry.

While the Rishi and she were living there, the twin Ashvani Kûmár (that is to say the celestial doctors of Indra's heaven) visited this place on a pilgrimage, and became the guests of the Rishi, and complained to him that Indra had prevented them from taking their share of the sacrifices. The Rishi said that if they would restore his eye-sight and make him young again, he would intercede with Indra, and reinstate them in their rights. They agreed, and advised the Rishi to construct the reservoir now known as the Chyavan Kûnd. He did so and bathed there, and was restored to youth, and recovered his eye-sight. The Rishi then performed a sacrifice and invited all the gods, including Indra. Then he begged Indra to restore them their rights, and eventually Indra consented. There is a temple of the sun at Sûtrápádá with an inscription dated Sumvat 1357, A. D. 1301, to the effect that Vejaldeva Bûta established the image of the sun. This Vejaldeva was probably one of the Wájás of Somnáth Pátan. This portion of the coast from Mádhavpore to Jáfarábád is called Nágher, and is very fruitful and abound in water. The following couplet is said by the seacoast people regarding Nágher:—

वाजा ठाकर ने अंब वन, नार पदमणी घेर ॥
रैंट खटुंके वाडीये भोय लीली नाघेर ॥

Where there are Wájá Thákores and mango-groves and Padmanis dwell in the houses. And Persian wheels creak in the fields that land is green Nágher.

The ancient temple of Kadwár, about two miles to the W. N. W. is well worth a visit, and is probably more ancient than its more famous neighbour. It is said to have been built in the reign of Nand Rájá of Magadha, whose brother-in-law and viceroy Ráodráksh ruled at Júnágadh. The temple is that of Varáha the 3rd or boar-incarnation of Vishnú. There are 3 images in the temple, viz., (1) of the Varáha incarnation, (2) one of the Narsingh incarnation, and (3) one outside which is of the Wáman or Dwarf incarnation. The population consists chiefly of Áhirs, Rajpûts, Kolis and Dheds. There are also Wâniás, Bráhmans, Kunbis, and Mûhammadans of different classes. The kolis are principally of the Gheria subtribe. The entire population by the census of 1872 was 2,950 souls, but it is diminished to 2,857 in 1881 owing to the famine of 1878-79. There is a roadstead at Sûtrápádá, but few vessels touch here, and there are none belonging to the town, but of late years, owing to the erection of a cotton press, some cotton has been exported from Sûtrápádá. After the Moghal authority became weak in the peninsula, Sûtrápádá was seized on by its Múhammadan garrison, but they were eventually driven out by the forces of the Nawáb of Júnágadh in whose hands the town remains.

Túlsishâma.

Tûlsisháma, about twenty-one miles north of Úná, is situated in the Gir forest. There are seven kûnds filled by a spring of warm water (outside the temple), in the seventh of which the lower castes bathe. The six other kûnds are reserved for the higher classes. This water is fairly warm probably from about 70 to 80 degrees Fahrenheit. The name of the place in the Pûránas is Taptodak or the place of warm water. Thus the Prabhása Khaud has the following Shloka :—

तप्तोदके नरः स्नात्वा तलस्वामिनमर्चयेत्

"A man should bathe in Taptodak and then worship Tal Swámi." Tûlsisháma is said to derive its name from Krishna, who slew Tal Daitya here, and is hence worshipped as Tal's lord Talswámi, whence Talswám, Talshám, and finally Talsi and Tûlsishám. Others say that Tûlsi was the wife of Jálandhar Daitya otherwise called Shankh Chûd, who resided in Div island, which is from this cause called Jálandhar Bet This Daitya had received this blessing from the gods, that so long as his wife should remain chaste he should be unconquerable, and he commenced to be in consequence very tyrannous, and even threatened the palaces of heaven. The gods then came forth to war with him, and after the other deities had suffered defeat, Shiva himself came to combat with him, but was unable to prevail. Finally, Krishna assuming the form of her husband, came to Tûlsi, and thus by deceit enjoyed her. The charm was thus broken, and Shiva killed Jálandhar Daitya. Tûlsi then became a Sati and burned with her husband on the funeral pile, but ere dying, she cursed Krishna for his deceit and changed him into a Sháligrám stone. Krishna, however, bore her no malice, but vowed he would marry her, and changed her hair into the Tulsi plant and herself into the Galki river in which these stones are found. On Kártik sûd 11th the Tûlsi plant is married to the Sháligrám stone by Hindus. As it is said that it was here that Krishna met Tûlsi, the place is called in memory of them Tûlsishám.

Úná and Delwáḍá.

There are many reasons for taking these towns together, one being their propinquity, but they are always also coupled together in common parlance. It would seem that the ancient town of Úná was called in Sanscrit Únat Dûrg (the lofty fortress), and that it was situate close to the present Úná, which was then known under the name of Delwáḍá. Hence Úná-Delwáḍá were in those days almost synonymous. It is situated on the bank of the river Machûndri. In former times Úná-Delwáḍá was ruled by Únewál Bráhmans, but on a certain occasion they offered an insult to the bride of Vejal (Vinjal) Wájo, who surprised the town, and put them all to the sword, and himself assumed the government. But as the ancient Úná or Únat Dûrg, which was the residence of the Bráhmans, was considered defiled by the slaying so many of their sacred race, Únat Dúrg was suffered to fall waste, and the population moved into the adjacent town of Delwáḍá, which was hereafter called Úná. Some years afterwards when Úná had fallen under the Mûhammadan rule a new town was founded about three miles south of Úná on the Machûndri river, and to this town the old name of Delwáḍá was given, and though the Mûhammadans called it Nawánagar (the new town), the name of Delwáḍá has stuck to it. Vejal Wájo did not long retain his conquest, and the place was conquered by the Mûhammadans. Under the Sûltáns of Gûjarát Úná-Delwáḍá were of much importance from their proximity to the island fortress of Div, a point of great importance for the defence of the Gûjarát shipping, and from which Delwáḍá is about 4 miles and Úná seven miles distant. Malik Eiáz, the great governor of Sorath, had his principal residence at Div, but frequently resided at Úná, and he is mentioned in the Sanskrit inscription of Samvat 1582, A.D. 1526, in the tank at Úná, and his grave is shown in the mausoleum of Hazrat

Sháh without the town of Úná. After the dissolution of the Moghal power, Úná-Delwáḍá, like most of the towns on the seacoast, fell into the hands of the Mûhammadan garrison, who thenceforth were independent, sometimes however acknowledging the authority of the Júnágadh Nawáb, and sometimes of the Habshi of Jáfarábád. They were, however, finally subdued in about A. D. 1782 by the Nawáb of Júnágadh, who now owns these towns. There is a celebrated inscription in the Sháh Bágh at Úná, dated St. 1652, on the 5th of the dark half of Kartik, equivalent to A. D. 1596, in memory of Jagat Gûrû Hirvijaya Sûrishwar. This inscription mentions how the Emperor Akbar abolished the pilgrim tax at the Shatrûnjaya hill, and also repealed the jazya and other levies. Nawábandar is the port of Úná-Delwáḍá, and is capable of much improvement ; at present its trade is confined to local wants. It is situated about four miles S. S. E. of Delwáḍá. The population of Úná and Delwáḍá by the census of 1872 was 7,056 and 3,079 souls respectively, but they were reduced to 5,980 and increased to 3,373 in 1881.

VEJALKOTHÁ.

Another famous place in the Gir is Vejálkothá or Vejalkot, which is a height on the eastern bank of the Ráwal river and flanked on one side by this river and on the other by the Sûrtali stream. It is entirely surrounded by these streams and other ravines save at the two gateways which lie north and south. The position is very strong, and it was a famous stronghold for outlaws in ancient times. Near Vejalkothá on the opposite bank of the river Ráwal is a small arched gateway of brick lying at the foot of the Khábrá hill, and hence called the Khábrá Gate. It is evidently part of some very ancient building. Vejalkothá is said to have been named after Sarvaiya Vejá, who, with Jasá, his brother, were originally Grásiás of Amreli. Expelled thence by the Mûhammadans, they settled Jaso at Jesar and Vejo at Háthasni in Únd. Jealousy, however, sprung up between them, and Vejo treacherously slew Jasá's son Ranmal. Then fearing Jasá's vengeance, he fled to the Gir Forest, and lived in this deserted stronghold. But Jasá pursued him, and camped at a spot now called after him Jesádhár. Here Vejo, who was not aware of Jasá being so near, accidentally went while hunting a boar. When Jasá captured Vejo, he put arms in his hands and told him to defend himself, but Vejo hung down his head and said that his guilt in treacherously slaying Ranmal forbade him to take up arms against Ranmal's father. On this Jasá slew him, and this deserted fortress has ever since been called Vejalkothá. Others, however, attribute the founding of Vejalkothá to Vejal or Vinjal Wájá. But the appearance of the place is even more ancient than Vinjal Wájá's time, and it probably was founded by dynasties anterior to either Sarvaiya Vejo or Vinjal Wájá. Vejo Sarvaiyá's stay there, was enforced and temporary, so that, though he may have taken shelter there, it is not probable that he could have built it. Vinjal Wájá is much more probable, only the buildings seem to date from at least A. D. 800, whereas Vinjal Wájá could not have been anterior to the 14th century A. D. Until a more elaborate examination has been made of Vejalkothá, it will be difficult to assign it any accurate date. but it will probably be found to be certainly at least as old as A.D. 1,000.

Verát, Chitrod, Kankái, etc.

Verát, Chitrod, Kankái, &c., are old villages now deserted, or else merely occupied by a few huts of Chárans, Rabáris or other cattle grazers, but which evidently must once have been large and populous villages. Near Máliá also are many waste sites with ancient pályás or memorial-stones. These villages were probably once inhabited by Káthis, who were driven out in the 14th century Samvat by Rá Khengár III. The most ancient of all of these was doubtless Kankái, which was built of brick both the fort and the temples and houses therein. The temples of the Kankái Mátá and Káliká Mátá are, however, built of stone, but they have been both probably recently repaired. The temple of Kankái, Mátá, who is the tutelary goddess of the Kapol Wániás, contains an inscription to the effect that it was restored in St. 1864 / A.D. 1808 by Kapol Wániás, Gándhi Kiká and Devsi Raghunáth. Kankái is probably contemporaneous with Valabhi and other ancient towns, and probably dates as far back as A. D. 500, if not older still. It is situated on the bank of the Singavdá river, about ten miles south of Visáwadar.

Chitrod.

Chitrod is on the eastern bank of the river Hiran, and is also ancient but probably much more modern than Kankái. It is said to have been governed by a Rájá named Hathisingh, who was the ancestor of the tribe of Háttis.

Verát.

Verát is about coeval with Chitrod, and is supposed to have been ruled by the Chávadá Rájpûts, but this is mere tradition. It is also called Verát Nagri; other ancient places in the Gir are Hiraniu, probably the modern Tálálá, where there are the remains of a mason's band yet visible. Ambát, near Jamwálá and Ghátwad, is surrounded by a singular excavation cut in the solid limestone. This was probably an irrigation channel, the Bhim Chás in the eastern Gir near Chikal Koba seems to be a channel cut in the rock for the conveyance of water for irrigation or other purposes. The hamlet of Bhim ká Dewal or Bhim's temple is about fourteen miles east of Pátan Somnáth, and the temple is a fine and ancient one. Other noticeable places in the Gir are Chhelna, Sásan, and Mandor. Chhelna in the centre of the Gir was no doubt formerly cultivated land; numerous wells are to be found in its lands, and it probably fell waste in the troublous times early in the 18th century, and its land were overgrown with forest. Mandor, where there are some Buddhist caves cut in the bank of a stream which joins the Hiran, probably fell waste about the same time. It is about nine or ten miles north of Sûtrápádá and five or six north-east of Pátan Somnáth, and must have been a fine and flourishing town. There are about six caves in the bank of the affluent of the Hiran, and one cave in the bank of the Hiran itself. The town of Mandor lies in the fork between the Hiran river and its affluent. The town was surrounded by a fort wall of cut stone and had a handsome gate. It is said to have belonged to the Háttis.

Verάwal Pátan.

Veráwal is known in the Puránas as Veláwan or the forest of creepers; but three other derivations are suggested, one from Velákúla, a term used in old inscriptions for a small port. Thus in the inscription in the temple of Harsadh Mátá the words occur "Hûrmûz Velákúll" *i.e.*, port of Ormuz. Another is suggested from the tradition that Seláit Wála married a wife from this part of the country and stayed here for a time: afterwards his son Dhána Wála succeeded him on the Talája Gádi and his son Veráwalji came hither and founded the village of Veráwal. A third derivation is from "Viláyasthal" or "charming place." It has owed its origin to its celebrated neighbour Pátan Somnáth, and rose into notice as a port principally during the time of the Gûjarát Sultáns, when and afterwards until superseded by Surat, it was the principal port of embarkation for Múhammadan pilgrims to the sacred cities of their faith. It seems to have fallen waste at one time, for the Diwan Ranchodji's history tells us that Mámet Khán Lodhi held Pátan Somnáth and other places in Jagir from the Gújarát rulers, and that he peopled Veráwal in the middle of the 18th century A. D. He also mentions that later on in this century Mánáji Ángria sailed hither and attacked Veráwal, but, after fighting for three days and nights, was forced to depart after receiving the present of a horse. He also says that the Portuguese of Div made several fruitless attacks on Veráwal. Kázi Shekh Mia of Mángrol conquered Veráwal in about A. D. 1762, but in a short time it was wrested from him by Diwán Amarji of Júnágadh. Still later on in A. D. 1787 Káná Súltánji of Porebunder conquered Veráwal and retained it for two years, but Nawáb Hamid Khán of Júnágadh reconquered this town in 1789, and since then it has remained in the possession of Júnágadh. In the temple of Harsad Mátá (classically Harsidh) is the celebrated inscription of Samvat 1320: this inscription is specially notable as recording the fact of a Múhammadan endowing a mosque in this year. And it also bears four different eras, namely, those of Vikram, Sháliváhán, Valabhi, and Shri Singh. It is from this inscription that it was discovered that the Valabhi Samvat commenced in A. D. 319, and that the Shri Singh era dates from A. D. 1113. The river Devká called in the Puránas Deviká flows to the north of Veráwal, and finally bending to the west joins the sea near the Jáleshvar temple. This place is called the Dani Bárû. The Jáleshvar Mahádev is situated by the seashore on the northern bank of the Dani Bárû, and derives its name from the word "Jál," a net, as the legend relates how the fishermen of Rájá Nábhág accidentally caught the Ápastambh Rishi in their net, and he becoming indignant cursed them and their Rájá. Afterwards on their Rája professing his sorrow and presenting the sage with a cow, he was forgiven through the intercession of another sage Lomash Rishi, and the ling which had been adored by the Rishi has ever since been called the Jáleshvar Máhádev. The fishermen also expressed contrition, and attained salvation, and the fishes were restored to life and became immortal. It is about two miles distant from Pátan Somnáth, and is a convenient port of call for steamers passing between Bombay and Karáchi or Kachh. But the sea is so violent on this coast after the middle of April, that this added to the fact that there is neither safe nor deep anchorage near the shore, prevents its being resorted to by any but local shipping of small tonnage. During the hot weather small boats making the shore from the mail steamer, which anchors about three miles out, are sometimes liable to be capsized. Small steamers come in somewhat nearer. The late Nawáb has spent some money in improving the port and erecting a light-house, but in truth without large expenditure, it will never be anything but an indifferent port or roadstead. Veráwal is famous for its onions, which are large and mild like Spanish onions, and are largely exported. It exports cotton, and imports grain, piece-goods, and timber. The population of Veráwal according to the census of 1872 was 10,725 souls, but in 1881 had increased to 12,111 owing to increased briskness of trade.

VISÁWADAR.

Visáwadar, about twenty-five miles S.E. of Júnágadh, is situated to the north of the Gîr Forest, and used to be the head-quarters of the Harsûrka Káthis, who formerly enjoyed great possessions in these parts. The town is surrounded by a fort. The climate and the water are both unhealthy. The river Popatri flows by Visáwadar. Its water is supposed to be very prejudicial to health. There is a famous couplet regarding this :—

पोपटडी कहे हुं पातली, हालुं धरती हेठ.
पेहेलां नाखुं खाटले, पछी बधारुं पेट.

The Popatri says I am shallow and flow beneath the earth.
First I cause people to take to their bed, and then I cause their stomach to swell.

A swollen stomach is one of the symptoms of illness caused by drinking Gir water. The population, according to the census of 1872, was 1,029 souls, but decreased to 924 after the famine of 1878-79. Visáwadar is the chief town of a mahál or revenue division, and a Wahiwatdár (or Revenue official) and a 1st Class Magistrate have their head-quarters here. Six miles to the east of Visáwadar is the Hothaliá Hill, wherein is the cave of Hothal Padmini, a famous character in local legend. She, when her father was dying and her brothers flinched, vowed to avenge him on his enemy Bamánio Bádsháh (Jám Bámanio) She assumed man's dress and armour and met with a Rjput called Odhá, who was also marching against Báranio. Odhá had been banished from his countr' of Kachh by his brother Tamáchi on a false complaint from his wie Minaldevi that Odhá had outraged her modesty, the truth being that he had refused her advances. In this strait he sought shelter with his cousin Visalde Vághela of Wadhwán, and observed that Visalde mingled dust with his food, and on enquiring the reason, was told that it was because of the wrongs he had suffered fom Bamanio Bádsháh. Odhá and Hothal performed many exploits together, and finally one day when Hothal was bathing alone in a tank, Odhá accidently went there and perceived that he was a woman. Then Odhá married Hothal, and she resided in this cave in the hill now called after her name. Here she bore him two sons, named Jakhro and Jesal. After twelve or fourteen years spent thus Odhá felt home-sick and begged Hothal to accompany him thither. She said, "It is not advisable that we should go thither, nevertheless if you wish it I will accompany you on condition that you will never divulge that I am Hothal Padmani." He promised her, and they returned to his village. Her sons were so brave and gallant that they slew a lion who had much annoyed the village. The villagers then enquired who his wife was to have born such gallant sons. Odhá at first hesitated, but finally when pressed confessed that she was Hothal Padmani. When he returned home Hothal reproached him for what he had done, and taking Jesal with her departed to her cave. Odhá begged her to stay, but she refused, but promised to return on Jakhro's wedding day, if he would light a piece of incense which she gave him, and think of her.

When Jakhro was married, he lighted the incense, and immediately Hothal appeared bringing with her his son Jesal. Jesal was married also at the same time as Jakhro, and after the marriage Hothal departed alone for the cave. Odhá followed her at a little distance, until she entered the cave, but when he arrived there he found her not, and it is conjectured that she was an Apsará who had displeased Indra, and had therefore been banished from Swarga until she should have taken on her a human incarnation and married a mortal. Now that her sons were married, her earthly mission was accomplished, and she was caught up to heaven. Odhá remained till his death seeking and lamenting for Hothal. Her cave is called Hothal Padmani's cave to this day, and the hill also is called the Hothalio.

WÁMANÁSTHALI, THE MODERN WANTHALI.

This town, which is the principal town of the parganah of the same name, is situated about nine miles to the west, south-west of Júnágadh. It lies in 31° North latitude and 70° 30' East longitude. The name Wanthali is said to have been corrupted from the ancient name of this town, which was Wámanásthali or the abode of Wáman. In the Wanthali Raustambh, dated Samvat 1469 / A.D 1413 it is called Wámanpûr. In the inscription in the Háníwáo at the village of Dhandhúsar it is called Wámandhám, but in the Kûmárpál Charitra, &c., it is called Wámanásthali.

It was also sometimes called Devasthali, which name was corrupted into Dethali. The population of Wanthali, according to the census of 1872, was 6,056, and according to that of 1881, 6,529 souls. Wanthali is at present famous for its coppersmiths' work, also its ironsmiths' work, and vessels, &c., made by them are exported to the neighbouring towns and villages. And Dhotis, Pachhedis, and other clothes are woven here for native wear. The town of Wanthali is famous from ancient times. The Girnár Mahátmyasár says that a famous wise and excellent Daitya reigned at Balisthán (Bilkhá) named Bali Rájá, who was about to celebrate his 100th Yadnya, in each of which he sacrificed a horse. Now, as it is understood, that who ever may be able to perform 100 Ashwamedha sacrifices will attain to the throne of Indra. The gods were therefore much alarmed, and implored Vishnû to protect them. He consented and became incarnate as the dwarf Wáman. Now Bali Rájá was very generous and never refused charity to any one. Wáman the dwarf went to Balisthán, and arrived when Bali Rájá was distributing charity to the Bráhmans during the performance of this sacrifice. Bali Rájá was attended by the Daitya Gûrû Shúkráchárya. Shûkráchárya perceived by his wisdom that Wáman was a god in disguise and warned Bali Rájá not to listen to his request. But Bali Rájá refused to deny the request of the suppliant dwarf. Wáman then asked for three paces of land, and Bali Rájá assented. Bali Rájá was pouring water into the dwarf's hand by way of confirming his gift, when Shûkráchárya, assuming an infinitesimal form, entered the spout of the vessel from which Bali Rájá was about to pour water in order to prevent the gift being confirmed, and no water issued. On this Bali Rájá pushed a blade of Kûsha grass up the spout to clear it. This pierced Shûkráchárya's eye and he fell out from the pain and the water flowed forth. To this day one-eyed people are called in jest Shûkráchárya. But the gift was now confirmed. Wáman then assumed a gigantic aspect, and at one stride covered the earth and at the second the heaven. He then said to Bali Rájá, "Where shall I plant my third footstep." Bali Rájá recognizing his divinity offered his head humbly for the third footstep. Wáman then was then in the semi-independent charge of Súrat and Kambay. Afterwards an affray occurred between Haidar Kúli Khán's troops and those of Safdar Khán and his relatives, owing to some trifling dispute about a water-carrier, and the Bábis were forced to take refuge at Pálanpur; but afterwards, through the mediation of Muhammad Firoz Jálori of Pálanpur, a reconciliation between them and Haidar was effected, and Safdar Khán was appointed deputy governor of Godhrá. At this time his son Salábat Muhammad Khán appears to have been governor of Viramgaum, and Jawán Mard Khán governor of Rádhanpur, while a son of Salábat Khán's, named Muhammad Bahádur, was foujdár of the districts immediately around Áhmadábád and afterwards was appointed in about A. D. 1722 to the charge of Sádrá and Virpur in the Mahi Kánthá with the title of Sher Khán. Haidar Kûli Khán, one of the leading men of the time, was in passes through its lands. It is about nine miles south-east of Kúndlá. The name is said to be derived from Gátra (body) and Gadá to bury, because Báwá Somnáth of Gorakhmadi buried himself alive here. The Káthis of Gádhakdá had carried off his cattle. The Báwá accordingly went to Gádhakdá and demanded their restoration, but the Káthis refused. After waiting for three or four days fasting he dug a grave and descended therein. On seeing this the Káthis remonstrated with him and offered to come to terms, but he replied, "When an ascetic has once entered the grave, he may not return." Then he cursed the Káthis and said that they would never be prosperous in future, and then caused himself to be buried alive under a banyán tree still called Somnáth no Wad. Chomlá Khumáṇ of Gádhakdá distinguished himself by recovering some cattle of Júnágadh villages from the Khasiás of the Bhávnagar village of Sedardá. The population but he was no match for Nizám-úl-Múlk, one of the first of whose measures was to appoint Safdar Khán Bábi as his deputy. The Bábis who had never quite forgiven Haidar's first warfare against them, and who somewhat feared that should he attain to supreme power in the province he might despoil them of their estates, at once ranged themselves on the side of order and the Nizám, and their example, added to the general distrust felt for Haidar, and meanwhile granting Sher Khán leave to visit his jágir at Goghá secretly directed him to proceed thence to Júnagádh to take up his appointment. Sher Khán accordingly at once proceeded thither and relieved Mir Dost Ali and took into his employ all that officer's troops and established himself so firmly that Mámú Khán found it advisable to withdraw his pretensions and retire. At this juncture Hazabar Ali Khán died and the emperor nominated in his stead Himat Ali Khán, nephew of Momin Khán, to the foujdári of Sorath, and Himat Ali wrote to his uncle to procure for him a fitting deputy. As the Máráthá incursions increased yearly and as Sher Khán Bábi was able to hold his own with them, Momin Khán confirmed him as deputy.

In the meantime the Maráthás continued their incursions into the peninsula with more or less success, and Rangoji established himself at Borsad, and thus the Maráthás could enter either by way of Viramgaum or Borsad. Sher Khán conducted the management of Sorath with much judgment, and while strengthening himself in Júnágadh and the immediate vicinity, yet contrived not to draw on himself the enmity of the Maráthás; and specially he contrived to conciliate Rangoji.

In 1743, Momin Khán died, and Fidá-úd-din Khán and Momin Khán's son Múftakhir Khán received an imperial order to carry on the government of Gújarát until a new viceroy should be appointed. Rangoji now conceived the idea of seizing on the government, and with this idea he invited Sher Khán to join him. Sher Khán who saw in this invitation a means of furthering his own ambition, at once proceeded to Borsad, and commenced plundering some of the Kambay villages. Rangoji offered Sher Khán the post of deputy viceroy should he be successful, and made some futile attempts to assassinate Fidá-úd-din Khán and Múftakhir Khán, but these nobles joining their forces marched against him, and succeeded in detaching Sher Khán from his alliance. Rangoji was now defeated and eventually agreed to surrender both Borsad and Viramgaum, Sher Khán becoming his security.

Sher Khán was now in a very powerful position, he had befriended Rangoji, who was unaware of his treachery, while he had there; but while the flood lasts, it is fierce. It is said that a Cháraniáni was coming to Júnágadh with her babe in her arms during the rainy season. When she reached the town she found the Kálwah in flood, but ventured in and tried to ford the stream. She was however carried off her legs, and her child was washed out of her arms and drowned. She managed however to reach the opposite bank. Here she turned and cursed the stream and said,

कान्चळीमां कुर अने काळवानुं पुर.

The flood of the Kálwah shall be as scanty as the rice given to ascetics in a cocoanut shell.

There is a tradition that at one time certain Nágori Múhammadans who were Thánahdárs of Wanthali took independent possession of it, but they were soon driven out by the Fouzdárs of Júnágadh. There is a long inscription in the Vinjaleshwar Mahádeva temple at Wanthali, from which we learn that Kshemánand of Wanthali, son of Arisingh and father to Vijayánand, married Premaldevi, daughter of Vira Dhawal, son of Lavanaprasád the Solanki of Pátan. Vijayánand, his son, married a Ráthor lady, daughter of Údal Ráthor, friend of the above Lavanaprasád. Údal Ráthor had a son named Jaitra Singh, who had a son named Bhimsingh. This Bhimsingh is mentioned as being a friend of the Great Visaladeva Wághelá of Anhilwádá Pátan. Bhimsingh had a daughter named Minaldevi, and her daughter was Nágaldevi, and she was the favourite Ráni of Vijayánand of Wanthali. By Nágaldevi Vijayánand had two sons, Arisingh and Tejsingh, and two daughters, Hirádevi and Tárádevi. Of these two daughters Hirádevi was married to Lávanydhaval of the Chálúkya dynasty. At Hirádevi's death her mother Nágaldevi placed her statue in the temple of Vinjaleshwar. From another inscription at Wanthali we learn that in Samvat 1346, A.D. 1290, Vijayánand was the Mandleshwar or local chief of Wanthali, and that Sárangdeva of Anhilwádá was Lord Paramount. The Patel of Wanthali, by caste a Kanbi, is named Lakhmidas, and is a very wealthy man. His father's name was Ámbo. There are many mango groves near Wanthali, the soil of which is very fertile.

સંસ્થાન જુનાગઢ તરફથી મેહેરબાન કર્નલ જે. ડબ્લ્યુ. વાટસન સાહેબને યાદી વકીલ દફતર નંબર ૫૨ તા૦ ૧૫મી જાન્યુઆરી સને ૧૮૮૪ ની આપતાં તેઓ સાહેબે રાજ્યસ્થાનીક કોર્ટનાં નંબર ૩૭૧૭ તા૦ ૨૧મી જાન્યુઆરી સને ૧૮૮૪ મુકામ કુડાનો શેરો કર્યો છે કે સંસ્થાન જુનાગઢ તરફ શેરો બતાવી કેહેવું કે આપના તરફથી ગેઝીટીયર સંબંધી જે હકીકત મળેલ છે તેથી વધારે કેટલીક હકીકત અમે બીજાં પુસ્તકોમાંથી પણ લીધેલ છે. તો એ પ્રમાણે અમે બીજા પુસ્તકોમાંથી લીધેલ હકીકત અથવાં જે હકીકત આપે આપેલ નથી એવી હકીકત અમે બીજેથી મેળવી લખી હશે તે આપને બંધનકારક નથી. તારીખ ૨૧મી જાન્યુઆરી ૧૮૮૪. મુ૦ કુડા.

મેહેરબાન વાટસન સાહેબની અંગ્રેજી સહી.

“ખરો ઇંતેખાબ.”

હરિદાસ વિહારીદાસ,

મુખ્ય દીવાન, સંસ્થાન જુનાગઢ.